IF I WERE YOU

The Complete Guide To Thriving
In The Insurance Industry

PRESTON SCHMIDLI

If I Were You -- 1st ed.

ISBN 978-1-7938861-3-2

Dedication

To Lacey who has been incredibly supportive through this crazy journey and loved me even when it wasn't easy.

To my mom who taught me how to smile and keep my head up in the good and the bad. Who loved me in every moment.

To my dad who inspired me to pursue greatness in everything I do. I wouldn't be where I am without your direction.

To Gentry, who helps me learn more about grace and love every day.

To everyone who has made me laugh, you kept me alive.

Table of Contents

Acknowledgements

First, I would like to thank my family for the support throughout the years to help me get to where I am today. The love and encouragement kept me fueled for this journey. My #1 Lacey, you are amazing. Thank you for standing beside me and choosing to grow together every day. And to Gentry, who probably didn't know it, but inspired me so greatly when he would wear the shirts from our businesses with pride. That changed a lot of things for me.

My team deserves strong recognition – you all make this possible. Thank you McBilly, James, Darlene, BG, Gena, and Sam. You are all rockstars.

I also want to thank everyone who has pushed me to strive for something greater in life, and who extended an olive branch when there was nothing asked of me in return. You beautiful souls. The year that went into this book was spent over countless video calls with incredible friends who I only had the blessing of meeting in person one or two times, but felt like I have known them my whole life.

McBilly Sy, Nick Ayers, Bobby Stocks, Rob Sekel, Rachel Scott, Will Shaw, Marissa Dropulic, Kirk Chester, Dave Jackson, Wess Anderson, Christian Goss, Fernando Mercado, Chris Langille, Rick Dugmore, Grant Botma, Jason Cass, Bruce Gold, Zack Gould, Matt Naimoli, Austin Whitaker,

Cody Baker, Kevin Gillespie, Joseph M'Mwirichia, Nick Carpenter, Sydney Roe, Robert Adler, Peter Germanov, Mitch Miller, and all of the authors and coaches throughout the years who helped me grow as a human – in turn impacting my business.

Foreword
by McBilly Sy

What if you had a roadmap that can tell you exactly where you need to go and what you need to do to reach the level of success you want with your agency?

What if that map also identified the hurdles of consistently growing, the ups and downs of business, the challenges that other people in the insurance industry have faced, and show you the shorter and easier path to your destination?

Well, this book isn't that map. It's better.

This book is your personal guide that Preston, along with other industry leaders, curated and created to help you achieve your dreams in business and live your best life.

This book will not only help you identify where you need to go, but it will equip you with the tools and action steps you need to take to get there.

As a well-established White Label marketer, my team and I are the people behind the campaigns of hundreds of large marketing agencies nationwide. My agency creates and runs the ads for other large agencies across different niches from Insurance, to Mortgage, to Real Estate and Legal. And so it's imperative that I network and grow beside the most influential marketers that exist to serve the needs of these businesses.

I first met Preston through an online group of marketers and entrepreneurs, most of which were struggling to get by – and the ones that were getting by, were doing so at their clients' expense. In an industry that has a lot of people with hidden agendas who like to talk big game but are not able to back it up, I found Preston to be a breath of fresh air.

He has a very sincere vibe that has made me feel welcome and unguarded, like we've known each other since high school. At first, we were just exchanging ideas and sharing our own experiences and journey. We started to converse more frequently through Facebook messenger and video calls. Through our online conversation, we began a wonderful friendship and I have had the honor of getting to know an individual who is extremely passionate on what he does for Insurance Agents and Mortgage Professionals, and who has a thirst for knowledge and innovation.

One particular instance was shortly after we became friends in the marketing world. He had mentioned an organic strategy that he conceptualized from a few former ideas that he has had. He took action immediately and implemented with a "Take No Prisoner" type urgency.

I didn't think much of it until we had spoken two weeks later, to find out that this one strategy he conceptualized and carried out had helped him reach his best month in business. It was at that moment that I realized that this guy is special, and far ahead of the pack.

Since then, he has continued to innovate and is responsible for some of the most creative marketing insights and strategies that exist within the Insurance and Mortgage industries. You can do incredible things when your highest priority is improving the lives of others.

Having knowledge of marketing strategies and tactics is great, but they only truly matter when you take action and implement them. And even more important, implement fast and build upon them.

That is how you can separate yourself from the pack. Successful people are those that stand on the shoulders of giants. Learning from mentors and other successful individuals. True winners are the successful people that take those ideas and deploy them at whatever cost.

In this book, you'll be presented with profound knowledge and fundamental truths. Some of which might even challenge your current way of thinking and doing business. You'll learn how to increase your book of business, make more money while saving your time, and truly scale your agency from where it is now to where you want it to be.

It's in your best interest to embrace this.

This book is your guide and map, to serve you on this journey and not do it alone. Open your mind to new ideas but also have the courage to fulfill them quickly. And trust that these principles are based on real world experience of industry innovators and market leaders. I truly believe there are no better experts that you could take this journey with.

Thus you would truly be standing on the shoulder of giants.

Be hungry for experiences to win and to learn, keep an open mind and walk with your personal guide, your map in hand. You are about to embark on an amazing journey through this book. One that will help you arrive to your desired destination bigger, faster and with longevity.

Bon voyage.

-McBilly Sy

Introduction

Hey fellow agency owner – if you're reading this right now, I can assume that you want to know the secrets of successfully marketing your insurance agency so you can generate more revenue. The good news is that this book that you are holding right now will help you get there. But first let me tell you a story...

In 2018, I dedicated an entire year of my life to connect with the most intelligent people available to support the insurance industry – because I knew that it was what I needed to have the agency and life that I wanted. I also knew that I would be able to share this journey with you and have the opportunity to make a positive impact on your life as well. These people aren't just other insurance agency owners... we met with other marketers, with consultants and vendors who serve the industry... We were on a mission to find the most qualified people in the game.

We travelled all over the nation: Portland, Los Angeles, San Diego, Scottsdale, Salt Lake City, Philadelphia, New York City, Las Vegas, Buffalo, Cleveland, Seattle, Puerto Rico, Scottsdale, Austin, Sacramento, Oakland and San Francisco.

There were tons of late nights and early mornings, so many video calls with these strangers-turned-close-friends who would share some of their deep insights to make this book happen. In an industry that is progressively under pressure and attack, I knew that I had to connect with these people and document the entire journey – for all of us.

I would like to share a vulnerable moment with you though...

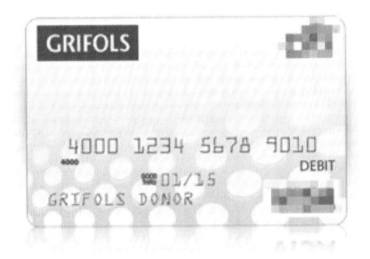

You might not know what this is, but not much longer than a year ago, this was how Lacey, my girlfriend, and I would pay for gas to get where we needed to go when the transition to being independent from a captive agency was happening. She would go to her job, and I would go to appointments. In my spare time, I would be at the food bank making sure we could put food on the table. We didn't have enough money...

If you don't know, this is a donor card (that's a nice way to call it). You get these when you sell blood at a plasma center...

We were completely lost in direction. Every morning I woke up feeling like I was in a car that drove off of a bridge into an ocean. The pressure built up around me, I felt trapped, I couldn't tell which way was up, and to be honest with you...

I was scared...

It was the most pressure I've felt as a man: To have a woman and a kid at home to raise, and try to set a great example for...

Every day it got harder to come home with that bandage on my arm...

Then one day, I quit...

I had enough...

I was sitting in the plasma center, and I broke down. Straight up weeping. I went from living in San Diego where I was blissfully happy, to coming back to Tacoma and ending up in that chair...

I remember thinking to myself, "How did this happen? How did I end up here? What did I do wrong?"

After that, I never went back. I cut up that card. And I swore that I would starve before I went back there...

You might be asking yourself, "Why are you telling me this?"

Because, maybe you feel lost. Maybe you're struggling to get by. Maybe you have lacked the direction you need to feel fulfilled in life...

And maybe I can share an honest and vulnerable moment with you that gives you hope...

We were just discussing donating blood in passing, and I realized (while it feels like it's been a long time now), it's only been a few years since we stopped going...

This was our best year yet – life is good and it will only get better. But it wasn't until I defined what my life would become - that I started to turn it around...

You are so close to the breakthroughs you want in life...

Burn your boats at the shore and keep moving forward...

There is no better time than now to draw your line in the sand, dig your heels in, and go to war for your dreams... Take no prisoners.

HOW IS THIS BOOK DIFFERENT?

The goal of this book is to help give you the blueprint and map to develop your dream agency. By the time you are done with it, you should be able to paradrop anywhere in the nation with nothing more than this book, a laptop and wifi and survive thrive in this industry.

We have written it very intentionally, and while you can read it in linear fashion from start to finish – we understand that you might be on a specific part of the journey that you need to focus your attention, energy and efforts in certain places.

With that said, we have broken it up into three sections. You will find the first section to be all about topics that generate revenue. The second will all be topics that are designed to help you have more time. The third section is about systemizing and building processes to allow you to consistently scale (and avoid the ups and downs of running a business). All three sections will help you make more money, save more time, AND build better systems and processes, but we categorized them by what they will do MOST for you.

So, dive in where you feel most compelled, and go where the journey takes you.

DISCLAIMER: While I have tried to make this book as timeless as possible, I understand some references to technology will eventually be dated. For a perpetually up-to-date list of services that are available to insurance agents go to www.ifiwereyoubook.com/resources and you will see them broken down by category. This way you will always have a shortcut to finding the best resources for your agency to grow.

For the new agent, flip to the next page – it's mandatory reading for you.

And for everyone reading – I wish you all of your desired success.

Survival Advice for New Agents (0-2 years)

Being a new agent in the insurance industry is incredibly difficult, and most people climb that mountain by themselves with no training or support – that's why I am so excited to provide you with the content of this book. You aren't alone anymore, and now you can learn from the wisdom of agents that have gone before you and made it to better days.

This chapter is chalked full of quick wisdom that you need to keep close to you. Those first 2 years require hardcore grit and perseverance. For a lot of us, these were the days of "Hamburger Helper without the Hamburger". I salute you for doing what most people aren't willing to do in life, to take the leap and build your parachute on the way down. That's how all amazing things are done. Below are discussions that I've had about how to get to month 25, because if you can get there – then your chance of survival increases drastically. You get to experience rotations of referrals, and now you are seeing your hard work pay off.

Getting to month 25

Keep overhead as low as possible:

"I consult with newer agents daily. #1 piece of advice is to keep expenses down. Go lean, lean lean and produce like no other. Once they hit renewals the tunnel fills with light." – Dave Jackson

When asked about what expenses Dave believes you should proactively avoid, he said, "Avoid the new shiny object syndrome. Stay laser focused on new sales and complete account rounding. I kept a list in my pocket of EVERY client with a Line of Business that I felt needed to be moved to me as a constant reminder."

This is a really critical point to get across. As you climb the mountain of success within Insurance, the trail is littered with the "bodies" of agents that spent more than they made (which is especially critical year 1), so you need to have a close eye on expenses and make sure that every dollar that goes out is with the implicit goal to make more money. I had discussed this topic with a few other successful agents, and below are some of their answers for you.

"Avoid ALL Debt – Cash Flow Everything Every Single Day"
– Brandon Smith

"Lean machine. Spend your money on marketing and what makes you money. Stop focusing on what everyone else is doing... Sales bring results" – Andy Priesman

IF I WERE YOU: Evaluate your expenses within the last 90 days. Go through each and ask yourselves if you truly NEED something to generate more revenue, or if it is a purchase you make out of fear of not having it, or fear of losing out. You'll find that most purchases we make don't have a direct impact on revenue, and those can be cut right away. Once you find out what you need, and then what you want, you can choose the priority of what to keep. It's important to play the long game, but you have to afford the short game long enough to get there too.

Keep your feet in the dirt (stay focused):

"Keep your pipeline in mind. If you spend all of your time working on that "one big account", then you don't have anything in the works for the next month's commission. Never slow down on getting that pipeline flowing" – Vonda Copeland

We all get excited on that first five or six-digit account that comes across our desk, and we spend an enormous amount of time trying to catch "the whale". But often times, you aren't the only person doing that, and only one person will close that account. In the time that you spend trying to catch the whale, you could be a diligent "fisherman" and make sure that you get a lot of smaller accounts. So make sure that you are cognitive of your time.

Another successful agent that I know, Cameron Brown keeps to the basics with raw wisdom, "Sell the hell out of your leads! Work 10, 12, 14 hour days, 7 days a week in the beginning! It will pay off!"

And sometimes, it's just about keeping it simple and accepting where you are at in your journey. As my friend Christian Moore shared with me for new agents, "Stop trying to learn insurance and learn how to create relationships. If you know how to create those, you'll learn how to get them to do what you want." It's easy to get stuck in the knowledge trap and feel like knowing more about insurance will help you get more clients. Makes sense on paper, but every minute you spend in a book or on the internet studying, is a minute away from a potential client. Use your first hundred or so clients as "paid training", and focus on meeting people. You'll learn the rest with time.

"Building relationships is going to be the foundation of your pipeline. Just because family and friends want to see you become successful, doesn't mean that they understand the commitment it will take to get there. Never give up or give in. Work like a slave the first year. Seriously." – Diana Perez

My friend Cameron Pechia shared some simple but actionable advice for new agents, "Set one in person appointment per week with a referral partner, center of influence or possible referral partner". To expand on this, challenge yourself to meet with a few referral partners every week. Create multiple revenue generating relationships and watch your growth accelerate.

IF I WERE YOU: Use websites like Zillow to find potential Loan Officer referral partners around you. Search for ones with great reviews, and reach out to them. Ask how you can help them in their business? Everyone tells lenders "I give great service, I do binders fast, and we have the best rates". That's the STANDARD, what makes you actually special to them? One thing most insurance agents don't do is ASK how they can help. They usually won't know how you can help right away because you are putting them on the spot by blatantly asking, so get to know them, build some rapport and ask questions about where the painpoints are in their business and find ways to help them solve those.

Keep your head in the clouds (Define your brand):

"If something isn't working, don't be afraid to change directions. Whether it's marketing, staff, your sales process, your niche, anything" – Shayna Levin

The beauty of being in your first two years is that you are a small business, your ability to change directions and try new things is at the highest that it will ever be. Anything that isn't working for you now should be something that you either improve or stop doing. You can't "keep grinding" if it's not working. You can grind your way into losing your business if you aren't super clear that what you are spending your time on is generating new business. It's also important to understand a caveat to this. That if you aren't willing to commit to something for at least 90 days, you shouldn't commit to it in the first place.

It's easy to make a commitment at the beginning, things are easy and we all love the idea of "new things" ... But it's in the middle of our commitments when we start to face resistance and experience the more uncomfortable times. You need to be willing to go through that. otherwise you'll always be chasing "the new thing" because you weren't willing to follow through with what you were already starting.

Another good friend of mine and very successful agent (who I interview in chapter seven) would always tell me "Everything you do has to point back to the mission". It's incredibly important to define who you are when you start your agency or when you are young. Give yourself an identity and a mission, that will give you a purpose greater than yourself. More importantly, it will give your staff and your clients a movement to attach themselves to. We all want to be part of something greater than us.

My advice is to ask yourself two necessary questions:

1. "What are three things I want our brand to be known FOR?"
2. "What are three things I want our brand to be known AS?"

The first question is action based, meaning they are things that you (or your brand) "do" or "have done". You might hear people mention your agency like, "They're the agency that specializes in XYZ" for instance. The second question is in regards to character traits, meaning ways people would explain you or your business. For instance, people might explain my agency 'Friends with Benefits' as an agency with a funny personality. It's a very simple example, but by drawing a line in the sand and defining who we are and what we are about – we give the right people something to latch onto and support. Strong branding gives people identity. People will wage wars and risk their lives for identity, don't underestimate its power.

If done right, this gives you the ability to future pace your dreams and actually start building your vision. As Josh Berg told me, you need to "reverse engineer the agency. Imagine how you want your agency to look in 5-10 years. Create processes and systems (write them down) as if you're at that point, even if you're the only one following them. It will make it easier to hire and hand off when that time comes"

Maintain your integrity (This is paramount):

You've come this far to build a business, always keep it within your mission to do this for the right reasons and in a moral way. There is so much business to be had, you have a special way to go after the market, you don't need to resort to anything immoral to reach your goals or dreams.

Aurora Mullet nailed it on the head when she said to me, "Always be the advisor and not the shark. Always have the best interests of your client first, even if that's not you. The integrity-based brand you build will feed you for life."

Mike Esparza shared some wisdom with me as well on this, "Don't allow product incentives to cloud your judgement. It may not be the best option for the client."

As you know – we are in a role that can make or break families in hard times, and when we make it our core mission to do our best for our clients within our business is when we tap into abundance mindset and truly start to thrive. Bruce Davidson really simplified this for us, "Maintain your integrity. All else will follow."

IF I WERE YOU: Define the things you would NOT do for money. Would you commit insurance fraud for a client? No? There's a good start. What else? Once you define the things you stand against, the things you stand FOR will start to become more clear. Then, back that up with your words and your actions – and before you know it, your entire business will be in full integrity with you.

Other advice:

"Hire slow, fire fast." – Justin Sloan

"Ask marketing reps what they have available for co-op money or forgivable (with production goals met) loan programs. These are great since they give you cash flow, which in many cases can turn into free money!" – Ryan Johnson

"For scratch agency owners: Set a 12-month goal for yourself. If you don't hit it, you need to ask yourself if you're a leader or an employee. Hiring someone is now the answer to failed plans. If you don't hit your 12-month goal, give yourself 6 months to hit another goal. If you fail again, fire yourself as your boss and go bring in a partner who can teach you how to be successful. Humility will get you places." – Christian Moore

"Know who you will be selling to and market them via social media and face to face. Also, build up referral partners." – Kelly Kemp

"If you're doing commercial – pick a niche (and stick to it)" – Eli Gillespie

"Have an attorney, CPA and financial advisor in your back pocket." – Michelle Mosher Rebhahn

"Choose the tools which will help you the most before going into business. i.e. AMS, Telephone, Automation and Rating System. Have processes in place for sales, onboarding, marketing, accounting and servicing the client. Know your products and the best fit [for your client]... it will save you a lot of time." – Donna Shearer

"My #1 piece of advice: ask around, locate and reach out to the 5 most successful agency owners in the country who have done what you want to do. Ask each for 30 minutes and come to each call with kick ass questions. What you can get from those 2+ hours will be instrumental in avoiding pitfalls and fueling growth for the future." – Matt Naimoli

Even when you don't have money, you need to respect your time like you do have money. Set a worthy self-valuation and work your ass off until that is the reality that you live in. Keeping a positive mindset during these first 2 years is what separates the people who look back and laugh at "the good days", from the people who look back during their lunch break of their 9 to 5 and wish they gave themselves a fair chance when they started their own business. So, keep pushing forward and heed the above advice.

Now you are ready for the rest of the book, but keep in mind – there will be mention of things that may cost money ahead. Keep a close eye on your expenses and focus your attention on what is proven to produce results. The shiny objects come and go, and you can play with them after month 25.

You may also see some things in the upcoming chapters that you can't afford NOT to have... I know that feeling very well... if you feel in your core that you NEED to invest time or money into something ahead, then listen to your instinct. Every one of the experts in this book kept going forward when everyone yelled to them "It can't be done... come back... you won't succeed", only to prove all of those people wrong... so while I want you to take our advice, I also want you to break through your own "4-minute mile" and show us all a new way to thrive in this business. So, onward, and keep crushing it.

PART 1
<u>MONEY</u>

"The man who stops advertising to save money is like the man who stops the clock to save time.
– Thomas Jefferson

"The simple truth is, if you aren't deliberate, systematically, methodically or rapidly and dramatically establishing yourself as a celebrity, at least to your clientele and target market, you're asleep at the wheel, ignoring what is fueling the entire economy around you, neglecting development of a measurably valuable asset."
– Dan Kennedy

CHAPTER 2

The Secret to Marketing in the Insurance Industry

Marketing is a hot topic for Insurance professionals. Every year the industry spends billions of dollars trying to compete for market space, while from the outside-looking-in, most insurance companies appear like crabs trying to get out of a pot of water... And in their pursuit to get out, everyone just continues to push each other down, to which it becomes a race to the bottom with who can have the lowest rate in town. In that game, everyone gets cooked.

In the pursuit of writing this book, I came across an old list of things that my girlfriend and I were brainstorming to do with the agency for the new year... this was back before I knew anything for what this book is about – which is important for you to witness. Because it shows that I wasn't any different than you or any other agent... I was trying to navigate to the best of my ability.

This journey has taken me from an insurance agent who happens to market, to a marketer who happens to sell insurance, and that was when my life exploded. My goal is to unplug you from 'the matrix' of how you've thought about selling your services. From here on out (if you can connect with this list at all), this book is going to feel really meaty and full of content. You will be introduced to a lot of new concepts. If you are struggling, and want help on this journey, you can always reach out to us at digitalnativesacademy.com to have coaching and guidance along the way. I believe in you, and we're here for the times you might not believe in yourself.

I'd like to share a personal mantra of mine I've kept close for years on this journey: "people seek price in the absence of value". If consumers are buying from price, that's because that's all that we gave them. So we need to go to the drawing board to develop the core of any successful marketing campaigns, before we talk about marketing theory and application. This is important to communicate to you, marketing will generally not be successful if the "offer" is not good. We can agree that we must have a strong marketing campaign (or series of campaigns), but we have to really understand what we are offering the consumer.

Creating the Irresistible Offer

What is an offer? Simply put, an Offer is the product or service that an individual or group of people give to another party in exchange for their product or service. Within the Insurance Industry we call this "Consideration". We agree to provide coverage, in exchange for a client providing "premium" among other things. It's simple. But when you think about how you want to position your services, you need to understand some of the core components of a successful or irresistible offer.

1. **It presents the outcome of your offer as obvious** – If your buyer can't easily visualize why you can help them in a way that a competitor can't, then you will often get overlooked. Your offer requires your buyer to be able to picture a better life with your services. You need to cut through the noise of the market.

2. **It removes the consumers pain and satisfies their deep desires** – Are you or your service truly solving a problem that the consumer has? Better yet, are you aware of the REAL pain that your customer is experiencing? If you aren't happy with your sales volume, but the sales you are making are due to "price competitiveness" then you aren't removing any real problem other than price. In their mind, you have become the least wrong answer, but that doesn't make you the RIGHT choice. Dig deeper on their pain so you can solve more than their rate dissatisfaction.

3. **It shows the value as outweighing it's perceived or real cost** – If your offer is good, price becomes much less of a driving force for the buyer to make a decision. In marketing we call this the "value stack". Your goal is to provide so much value to the buyer that they feel they are getting the better deal, and

that if they don't act now they may lose such an enticing offer. The more we can stack value, the lower the "perceived" cost is.

4. **It's message is centered around the active/engaged buyer** – Sounds simple, but most people try to target everyone so that they don't "lose anyone", but the act of pandering to everyone actually pushes away your consumers because they can't differentiate you from the market, making you invisible to their purchase decision.

5. **It uses social proof to further justify and simplify the decision** – People generally have a herd mentality, and will go where they see others go (and come back safely). This is biologically engrained into us. We want to be safe, and if we see that other people have used a product or service, and report good things, then it is "safe" to use. No one want's to be the man who discovered which berries NOT to eat.

6. **It gives a sense of belonging and identity to the buyer** – People need to feel needed, it is a fundamental desire of humans. If you position your product as an elite offer, that is exclusive to a group of people, they will defend it even when it is not the best option for them. For reference, look how USAA positions themselves. There are often prospects that

will be priced way higher with USAA but they will stay with them because they feel included into a culture of "exclusivity". USAA has done an incredible job of giving identity to their buyers.

7. **It contains a no-risk guarantee** – The less people feel that they have to lose when buying your offer, the more people will join you. So think about your products/services, what risks are there? Be critical, because your buyers are. Do you charge fees? If they cancel do they get a refund? What is your agency promise to them in the event of a claim? There is nothing wrong with charging fees, but everything should be positioned as minimal-to-no risk for them to purchase.

8. **It gives buyers a sense of power** – The consumer always wants to feel that they are buying and NOT being sold. Position yourself in an environment where they feel that they are the ones making the decision. This not only hits people's desire for power, but also their desire to feel right. It's one of the deepest desires that humans have. Humans are generally addicted to being correct. This also helps them feel noticed and understood. All of these are core desires of humans and should be intentionally satisfied within your offer. A simple way to do this, is to mirror the consumer's concerns back to them, and

tie in your product to each concern as the solution. Let them be the one to connect the dots that it solves their problem, and they will consider it "their idea" – increasing the likelihood they will buy.

Now that you know the 8 components of an irresistible offer, you can evaluate how you communicate your services to prospects, and establish how you are positioning yourself. Mastering these 8 things will make it so much easier to weave a winning message into your marketing. The cool thing about what we do as agents, is that "Our Offer" is a part of our entire agency. Our brand, our marketing, the policies we sell, the way we deliver them and make them available, our staff, ourselves... literally all of that is a part of what makes your "offer" attractive (or not). This is a great starting point for you to grow as an agency.

IF I WERE YOU: Struggling to come up with a great way to position the offer of your brand? Reach out and hire a branding/marketing company to guide you through the process. It's critical that you stay in your zone of genius – and when you are pulled away from that, hire someone who can help you so that you can get back to your zone of genius as soon as possible.

What happens after you get your offer? You buy leads, right?

One of the observations that we have seen in our marketing agency for Insurance Professionals is that leads are only one aspect to having a successful "offense". People that are generally looking for leads are trying to "fill a hole" in their business (which makes sense), but what we see is that it does not fill a hole. It amplifies whatever is already there. It's important to recognize that if you have leads, you no longer have a lead problem. Having leads just moves the bottleneck in your business and it's important to be cognitive of that. "Leads" are just one component of a thriving pipeline.

Before we go further, it's important to have an honest moment of self-reflection. When we talk about leads, this is a byproduct of marketing. But the addition of leads will NOT directly equate to an increase in sales. We often see two different responses to an increase in leads of an agency pipeline:

1. Group A has really dialed-in systems, which assists them in effectively building a relationship with their leads. These people see as if you could give them a phone book and they'd find a way to make more sales.

2. Group B is lacking in having strong sales systems and processes, so the leads seem like a burden. These insurance agents tend to end up spending MORE time and getting no results due to an increase in leads.

When you have a moment of honest self-evaluation on which group you are in, it will determine what you need to prioritize into your agency. If you find that you are in Group A, then keep reading as this chapter will help you feed the pipeline that you already have.

If you find that you are in Group B, (first of all, I appreciate your honesty. We all start somewhere), I recommend skipping forward to the second part of the book where we talk about how to gain more time. This section is really geared toward systematizing your agency, which will allow for you to have a more efficient and effective sales process.

Getting in Front of Your Audience

Let's dive into some marketing theory that is universally applicable to all forms of marketing, both traditional and digital. Since this book is about things I would do "If I were you", you won't hear much reference to traditional marketing strategies (direct mail, billboards, etc). I believe that it has it's place but one of the things that I love about digital marketing is the ability to simply and directly measure conversion at every stage. Also, if you know what you are doing digital marketing is WAY more cost-effective. You find out quickly what does or doesn't work with digital marketing, and you are able to get in front of the right people that need to hear your message.

IF I WERE YOU: Take this information seriously and apply it to your agency, you will be able to stand out from the competition and it will generate more results than anything you've done before – but you have to get your offer in front of the right people.

Now that your brand/marketing has a solid foundation of an offer, let's talk about "running traffic". When we refer to traffic, we are talking about the people that you are sending to your offer through some form of advertisement or branding campaign. For instance, if you have 100 people request a quote through Advertisement A, but Advertisement B only generated 10 quote requests, then Advertisement A would have generated ten times the traffic.

It's important to understand the three main types of traffic that exist:

1. **Traffic You Own**: These are people that are already on your email list or client list. Cross-sell opportunities are a great example of traffic that you own. The person has opted-in to your messaging, and you are able to directly communicate to them without paying for their information or to have access to them.

   Example sources of traffic you own: Your email list, people who like your social profiles, YouTube subscribers, current clients (For cross-selling).

2. **Traffic You Rent**: These are people that you are paying to get in front of. Normally we would call this "advertising" because when you rent traffic, you are paying another company for their data and potentially access to their platform. If you place an ad on Facebook for instance, you are renting their audience to get your message out. If the people don't opt-in, then you don't get to stay in front of them. Essentially, if you want to continue to market to this audience, you have to keep paying (unless they opt-in, in which they become traffic you own).

   Example sources of traffic you rent: Disruptive Advertising (Facebook, YouTube, Instagram, Snapchat), Search Advertising (Google, Bing, Yahoo, or other search engines), even Billboards or Direct Mail.

3. **Traffic You Don't Control (but can influence)**: These people you can influence from experience with you, but there is no way to fully control this. A good example is SEO (Search Engine Optimization) – you can create website/blog content that is better suited for people searching for keywords that would be aligned with your business, but there are variables also outside of your control at play. You don't own OR rent this traffic, you simply don't control it. You can however influence it through your brand and messaging.

Example sources of traffic you don't control: SEO or blogging, creating YouTube content, organic and publicly accessible social postings (like on your personal or business page on Facebook or LinkedIn).

The goal with traffic is ALWAYS to get to a place where you own it. If you are running ads, and you capture leads, it's imperative that you have systems in place on the back-end to stay in front of those people. The good news is that this book will go over multiple strategies to help you capitalize on your marketing efforts.

We just mentioned two of the primary traffic sources that you will use while marketing your business.

First is Disruptive Advertising: The goal of disruptive advertising is to interrupt the experience of the viewer with your message. A great example of this is an ad on Facebook that you see as you are scrolling through your Newsfeed. Odds are that the company advertising to you has leveraged the targeting options on Facebook and potentially infused their own data in with Facebook's targeting to get in front of you as a "Potential Buyer". Essentially you are going to the consumer to get in front of them.

Example of effective disruptive advertising: Mortgage company starts serving ads to people who are visiting websites like Zillow, Redfin or Trulia.

Next is Search Advertising: The goal of search advertising is pretty straight forward, you are bidding on keywords with other advertisers to get in front of people who are searching for those keywords. In search advertising, <u>the consumer is coming to you</u>. Some people prefer this strategy, but GENERALLY search traffic will be more expensive to generate – so while it may be "better" or "more qualified" traffic, it doesn't necessarily mean it is more profitable.

Example of effective search advertising: Person has a leaky pipe and fills their basement with 3 inches of water overnight. You aren't going to scroll through Facebook and hope you find a plumber, you are going straight to Google and searching for the most available plumber right now. I know, because I had to do this recently lol.

You might be asking yourself which is better for you, but it really depends on your goal. Every objective is going to have a potentially different marketing strategy. I would go so far as to recommend using them both in tandem. Gain the search traffic through a platform like Google for someone who has typed in keywords that you want to win, and then retarget them on Facebook, Instagram, YouTube, Snapchat, etc. That way you get in front of them when they search for you, and then you stay in front of them until they buy from you. This is called **Omnipresence** and it's one of the better strategies that we have seen our clients implement over the years. Generally, the more time and intention you are willing to put into your marketing, the better it will perform (but don't underestimate the power of simplicity either. It's always best to test what is working for your audience).

To know exactly what kind of advertising you need to use, or the message that you should have to connect with your audience, it's important to know where the prospect that you want to speak with is at on their journey.

One of my favorite copywriters Eugene Schwartz created an amazing breakdown on the stages that a person goes through on a journey to buy a product (or do anything in life really). He calls this "The 5 Levels of market Sophistication", but I've always found it easier to call it "awareness" instead of sophistication for this explanation.

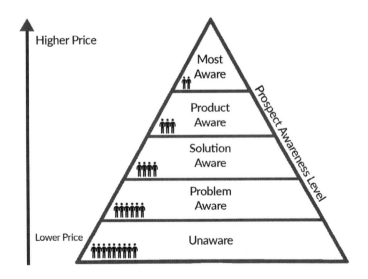

Level 1: Unware

At this stage, the buyer is generally unaware that they have a problem. Therefore they couldn't possibly conceive that you have a solution they need. They don't know you, they haven't heard of you, they haven't heard of your product and they haven't identified any problem you can solve. Most consumers will fall under this category.

Level 2: Problem Aware

This is when the buyer becomes aware that they have a problem, but they have no idea what the solutions are. They may have received a renewal statement with a huge rate increase, or maybe even they had a claim get denied and they started to question if they are properly protected. They have now identified the problem, but are still unaware of who you are, your products and services, and they don't know how you or your services can solve their problem. There are less consumers in this category than "Unaware", but it is still the second most populated group.

Level 3: Solution Aware

This is where the buyer becomes aware of the potential solutions to their problems. This is where you start getting into comparison shopping which is primarily price driven (because so many companies perpetuate that messaging). It doesn't have to be that way though. Whether it's on price, coverage or service – these consumers are now comparing you to the other agencies around bidding for their attention and business. So they are trying to make sense of all of the information at this stage. This is where you really get to peacock and stand out, because you want to be remembered. If you have an easy to digest presentation, especially if it's on video (which we take a deep dive into in the second part of the book), you will be off to a great start here. You can also see, since this person is aware that they have a problem and there are solutions that exist, you can have more direct and higher level messaging within your marketing efforts. There are slightly less consumers in this category than there are in the "problem aware" category. This is also where consumers get easier to convert into clients though since they are proactively seeking answers.

Level 4: Product Aware

At this level, the consumer is starting to look at products directly. Features and benefits. These buyers know that there are solutions to their problems, and they have even gone so far as to identify the specific products to help them. This is when a real evaluation for a purchase happens. This also is when you have the highest ability to position yourself as the best choice for them. Find ways to polarize yourself from the direct carriers, this will give the consumer something to latch onto other than price. Most agencies don't stand for anything publicly. So if you are willing to identify as a champion in their corner and let them know why, you have given them a cause to fight for. It even helps to vilify a competitor, but that doesn't have to be a person or a brand. It can be the problem that the consumer is experiencing that you vilify. This allows you to position yourself as the hero to their problem. Now when they think of the "solution", it has your branding on it. This will anchor you in their mind as the needed solution. This category is usually a much smaller demographic than the Solution Aware crowd because they're ready to make a commitment to a decision.

Level 5: Most Aware

Now the consumer knows your product, and most likely has or will buy your product. These people tend to become your ambassadors because they understand your services and how they solve their problems. You are the hero behind the solution, so these people will defend the brand and what it stands for because they were able to connect with it. By this point, you should have been able to ask for the sale and converted these people into raving fans. Then you can start to cross-sell them even more solutions to new problems that you help them realize, and put their fears to rest.

Often times I see agents doing their own marketing without formal training, what it ends up looking like is they are placing their message in front of "Unaware" or "Problem Aware" consumers, but they are speaking to them like they are "Product Aware" or "Most Aware". This makes it so that the consumer doesn't resonate with your message at all, so they never ascend up the levels of awareness.

I want to give you some real examples of messaging that you can use depending on where people are at so that you can understand and have context to this lesson.

Level 1: "Unaware" Example Headline

"Learn the 3 secrets your insurance agent doesn't want you to know (and why you SHOULD know)"

This makes them realize that there MAY be a problem in their life. This could be an article we write to get the consumer thinking about their insurance policies in a way that maybe they weren't already... it plants seeds of doubt in their current situation, which allows them to open up to the potential that they may need a solution, and now you can be the hero behind that. You'll notice that this makes no mention of me or my brand, because at this point it's not about us... it's 100% about the problem and the pain that causes the consumer.

IF I WERE YOU: Go to your local grocery store and fine the "Globe" or "National Enquirer" newspaper. These have incredible headlines and copywriting that is intended to suck the reader in to what you would otherwise not normally be concerned about. They trigger some deep human desires like a persons need to know something other people don't.

Level 2: "Problem Aware" Example Headline

"Don't buy insurance until you read this..." or

"Is your insurance protecting you? You may be surprised by the answer"

These headlines are starting to tap into their pains, which in our industry are fear based. The client is thinking "What if I'm paying too much?", "Do I have the right insurance policy?", or "Are we ACTUALLY covered when shit hits the fan?" These are fair questions, and the messaging that we have on the second level needs to speak to those concerns, those fears, those pains/problems.

Level 3: "Solution Aware" Example Headline

"If you just bought a home... you may be under-insured"

This could be a headline to an article from you or your agency talking about the lack of insurance new homeowners may have. This is an example that I like to use, because you could have written a blog article about "I bought a home, but do I have enough insurance?". You could track the people who read that blog and it's generally safe to assume that the people reading that article, more than likely just purchased a home. They are insecure about their policy. So by reading that article and THEN seeing an ad on Facebook that says "If you just bought a home... you may be under-insured", it allows you to confirm their suspicions and position yourself as their ally. You can talk about how YOU or YOUR AGENCY solve this problem for hundreds of local families every year, and how you are the trusted advisor to the community. This will help sway the consumer your direction.

Level 4: "Product Aware" Example Headline

"The XYZ Agency gave us the best service, and broke down our entire home policy to make sure that it had everything we needed, so that when there was a fire or something – we wouldn't lose what we worked so hard to gain. Thanks XYZ Agency! – Debra R"

Social proof is such a huge motivator because it triggers a tribal part of our brain that wants to feel safe. We want to know that we aren't the first person to buy a product... What if it sucks? What if we were wrong? Oh god, people HATE being wrong... Especially when that can have massive consequences. By showing that other clients happily work with you – you put your prospects fears to rest and it makes it much easier for them to share their payment details with you.

Level 5: Most Aware Example Headline

"If you know someone who has GEICO insurance... you may want to share this with them..."

These people are already clients most likely, so it's time to give them something to fight against or fight for. By using a strategy like this headline, you are making it much easier for your client to "refer" you to their friends, because you are telling them that if they care about their people, they will share this article with them. And all throughout the article, it is talking about the downfalls of a 1-800 agency and how you are the local advisor who has sworn against the low level of service you've seen so many people have from the direct carrier. By using a carrier's name in the article, you are creating a common enemy, and that allows you and your clients to position together against that common enemy.

You can see how there are different ways to communicate with these prospects in a unique way depending on where they are at in their journey. The more intentional you can be with your messaging in your blogs, your posts, your ads, and your branding – the more it will resonate with THE RIGHT people.

IF I WERE YOU: Use these marketing theory lessons for ALL platforms that you use. These principles of universal, and will work for how you communicate on Facebook (with ads OR organic posts), on YouTube, Instagram, and platforms that aren't even out yet). These are timeless concepts that if you truly understand and master, will make you an incredible amount of money and help you improve a lot of people's lives.

There's one final lesson that I think is paramount to you having a solid foundation in this marketing lesson. You may not have heard this yet, but the best way to get people to buy your product is to "Sell them what they want, and give them what they need".

On paper it sounds simple, but I want to break down what that means psychologically so that you can infuse this in your marketing from here on out.

People buy with emotion, and justify with logic.

You HAVE to understand this. The reason that the consumer is so price driven is because most agents compete on price, and that is the only thing that we ever give the consumer to base their decision off of. Price is logical. It's all numbers, it's completely unemotional. Hence the consumers frustration with the process. They will feel more comfortable making that decision on emotion than logic.

When you are trying to sell something on price, you are asking people to buy on logic, and justify with emotions. This isn't the way the human brain is designed. The emotions that people buy on are processed in the limbic part of the brain, or "Mammal Brain" as it is called. This is where people will feel that they did a good thing, and feel safer because of their decision. The part of the brain that justifies that purchase with Logic is the Neocortex, or "Human Brain". This is the part responsible for "reasoning and logic". So if we stimulate the limbic system first, and then give the neocortex reasons to "agree" with the limbic system, we have a solid sale.

Once you understand we are just rewording our marketing to appease the biological process for how humans interpret an offer or a message, this becomes much easier.

Let's go over two different examples to understand this concept:

Example A: "This policy has the best rate and the same coverage that you had before"

Example B: "This policy makes sure that when your house catches fire, or something else tragic happens, that your spouse and children will have all of your cherished possessions replaced, and you will have help transitioning into a new and safe home to raise your family in. We've made sure that this policy protects every concern you have communicated to us, which were very reasonable. You are properly protected with our policy"

Example A is pure logic, just numbers. Example B makes them FEEL secure. They feel safe, they feel protected. That is what they want from our services generally, and when we work with communicating the emotional aspects more, we allow them to buy for the right reasons for them.

CHAPTER REVIEW: Successful marketing is about connecting with where your prospects are at on their journey and connecting with them emotionally first, and then letting them use logic to cement their emotions for why to buy from you. When you do this, and have a well thought out and irresistible offer, you will be much better positioned to win.

UP NEXT: Now that you understand some of the core fundamentals of marketing, we will build on those principles to talk about using different media types and placements, and the future of connecting with consumers on the internet.

CHAPTER 3

Moving into the Future
with Nick Ayers

It's no secret that the insurance industry is antiquated and very behind the times. All the while technology is advancing at record rates, which induces a lot of fear for agents and agency owners. You hear terms like "insuretech" thrown around, and people are scared of disruption. But the beauty with being a small business is your ability to pivot in the face of change and adopt new systems and processes is so much greater than the large companies that are VC backed, and require board meetings to make the same changes. The change is inevitable and will take place whether we like it or not, but we can leverage change to our advantage.

I've always viewed this similar to the revolutionary war, and while the "redcoats" might have more money to throw at an initiative, our nimble businesses are still able to win the fight if we're willing to be creative. The original colonies didn't meet the British in the open fields where the redcoats stood, they fought from behind trees and other shelter – and would run to safety to reload and fight again.

Granted, we aren't in actual war, but every day is a battle of how you spend your time and the life you build for your future and your family. You don't have to keep standing in the open field, and do business "how it's been done". So, this chapter is about recognizing the weapons you have available to you in that movement. I am joined in this chapter by Nicholas Ayers of Made You Look Video Marketing to help arm your agency for success.

Let's dive into the different platforms that are available to you at as of now, and the different marketing and content strategies you can use to get your prospects attention and begin the conversion journey of turning them into paying clients.

Keep in mind, most advertising on the internet is done on an auction system. Some of the platforms mentioned here might be scoffed at today, but if no one else is advertising there, and competing to get their ads in front of the crowd – you may very well get great traffic for cheap since there is no one else in the auction. So before you turn your nose up at a source of prospects, run some tests there. It's okay if you aren't on all of these too. It's much better for you to do really well on a few than do mediocre on all of them. So, find what is best for you.

Where to Place Your Ads (Advertising Platforms):

The Giants

Google: There are two ways to use google as a business. The first is organically (through SEO, aka Search Engine Optimization), and the second is through paid ads (Now called Google Ads, formerly AdWords). Generally, lead quality is higher from Google if you are able to get it, since these people are actively searching for help. The cost is generally higher as well, since it can be a very competitive market for insurance.

SEO can be free if you know what you are doing, but it takes time, and if you don't know what you're doing then it can delay the process of getting results. With Google Ads you will generally pay more per lead, but depending on the market you are going after, it could be a vastly profitable campaign. Google does have decent targeting options and an ability to use a tracking tool to essentially mark the visitors to your pages so that you can easily retarget them for another ad (and generally much cheaper for the retargeting).

Facebook: There are a lot of ways to utilize Facebook as a business tool. Its flexibility is why this has become one of my favorite platforms to market with because they continue to innovate it with new methods of communication. You can get in front of prospects and clients through your personal page (I will always do this, since it's free and works wonders), and your business page (less appealing to me since business pages don't get as much love in Facebook's newsfeed algorithm, but this still can add value). Organically speaking, you can leverage groups like local BUY/SELL/TRADE groups to present yourself as the local expert for free, and that will get you business if you're starting out. You can utilize chatbots and other cool tools to integrate into Facebook Messenger.

The magic though comes in with Facebook's paid advertising. They have incredibly deep targeting options and the Facebook tracking tool (also known as the Pixel) allows for you to retarget people who visit your pages much easier on Facebook. The beauty of using these retargeting platforms is that when you use the Pixel in tandem with the Google tracking tool, you can start to build your data from one platform to the other and get a really high profile audience of people that are taking interest in your content (organic or ads).

To expand on the use of your Business Page earlier, there are still many benefits to having one (and you definitely should). It's not as much about posting on your business page for the engagement, because Facebook has pretty much reduced the exposure that you will get from your business page unless you put money into your posts (which I wouldn't recommend "boosting" just any post for engagement, you can do way better things than this to get people looking at you and save a lot of money). But by having a Business Page, you have a place for people to "like" and leave reviews.

This becomes much more important as people are considering buying from you, because they want to make sure that other people have had great experiences. So, the best way to use your Business Page on Facebook is to gather social proof. The more reviews you get, the better. Likes won't do much for you anymore, other than show clients and prospects that a lot of people like you – but that can't really be a bad thing either.

YouTube: As we continue on our journey into the digital age, video is becoming an increasingly important component to your internet presence – as you can use it to reinforce your blog posts, or store content for your website (maybe you want to have a video about your claims handling process, or store video reviews on your channel).

You can also advertise on their platform and YouTube (like Google, their parent company) has pretty effective targeting options, which allows you to get your advertisements in front of the desired audience, and communicate directly with them through one of the most effective methods of connection (video). We will be diving into video and YouTube a bit later in this chapter.

Instagram: As we continue to become more visually stimulated, we will continue to use platforms like Instagram. It is a huge platform for people who communicate visually, such as travel, cooking or lifestyle. But that doesn't mean that insurance agents can't get in there. Just like any other platform, if you have sufficient content and better yet, GOOD content – people will follow you. In response to YouTube and Snapchat advancements, Instagram has added a lot of video features which really expands the potential uses for the platform. Not only is it a great place to let people get an inner view to your business, but it's a fantastic place to advertise. Leveraging the same targeting options as Facebook since it is ran through the Facebook Business Manager, giving Instagram a lot of power for you to get your message in front of the right audience.

Showing Promise

Snapchat: While it is still a young platform, Snapchat shows a lot of promise for businesses to go to who work with the millennial audience. Having captivating content is critical here, but the advertising platform is really cheap right now as it's relatively new compared to the giants. But don't write it off, this could be a really big platform as time continues.

LinkedIn: A very underutilized platform as most people mainly use this as a digital resume, but it is a great place to get in from of a B2B audience. If you do commercial insurance, then this platform could be wonderful for you. Also, looking to grow your team? I wouldn't pass over LinkedIn then. LinkedIn continues to survive in the competitive marketing space, and I think they have the potential to roll out some really great marketing options in the future.

Pinterest: This most likely wouldn't be the best platform for a standard P&C agent, but if you have a niche market then this could definitely be for you. Like to insure the DIY crowd? Do you specialize in Wedding insurance? The audiences that gather here usually have some form of passion, so if you can speak to them with your agency, you'll be able to build a unique affinity with them that the competition can't.

Reddit: Definitely a less spoken about platform when it comes to advertising, but I think that we will be seeing more Reddit advertising in the future as brands test its waters. The interactive nature of Reddit users provides a higher engaged audience, which if executed properly could be very profitable to advertise with.

A lot of agents choose to be minimally present, choosing maybe one platform:

Some agents that want to turn the heat up choose multiple platforms to be on consistently:

The smart agents are not only using the proven platforms to get success, they are also using the tracking tools and Pixels provided to make sure they are in front of their ideal prospects everywhere on the internet:

IF I WERE YOU: If you are a young agency and your marketing budget is limited, focus on quality content and being consistent. That will definitely make a much more lasting impression than just advertising anyways. Challenge your capabilities, but don't spread yourself too thin, make sure you have the money and time to execute.

Nick: *"Whether we are using Facebook, or maybe we are using organic ranking on YouTube, whether we're using paid ads on YouTube, or we're just trying to get people to take action or make decisions on our website versus on something that they saw that was valuable... We have to ask ourselves what the frameworks are, and really try to approach it from more of a human psychology aspect. I remember when you [Preston] were filming your course, you really wanted structure to it, and I took a lot away from that. You have to show people why they're doing something, that way when something breaks they're going to know how to fix it. So taking that from you, I try to bring that into my course with a message of 'I don't want to just show you how to make a video. You can do that on YouTube. But how do we actually make videos that convert traffic', that is what we're building this on. The tactics will change, but the strategies apply to every platform, and always will."*

Regardless of the platforms that you are on, there are some things that don't change. One of the big things that you will see for every ad you run regardless of the platform, is the **creative** of your ad.

The creative is comprised of a few things:

1. What is the medium of the content: Still Image, Video, Slideshow, Just words? This is the first thing that your audience will usually see and it should be designed to capture their attention to read the headline.

2. What does the headline say? The headline is used to bridge the visual component of the ad to the body copy so that the reader/viewer can take the action you would desire them to. Headlines should generally be concise but engaging to invite the prospect in with as few words as possible.

3. Body Copy: Does the body copy of your ad make the prospect click through or complete the action that you want to make? Does it communicate in a clear fashion what they need to do to take advantage of your offer? Often times ads that convert poorly do so simply because the prospect doesn't know what to do or how to take advantage of the ad's offer. Having a clear Call To Action (CTA) is critical.

You can learn about headlines and body copy in a lot of copywriting books, and I would definitely recommend that you do this so that you can master effective sales copywriting, but for the purpose of this chapter – we're going to dive into the medium of the content, because there is a lot of opportunity here for agents like you to leverage tools like Video to make a really outstanding message to your audience.

Nick tells the story of when he started to re-evaluate the way he positioned his insurance agency to become dominant on the internet:

Nick: *"I was using video to figure out how to tell my story, as well as how I can enhance my skills to actually convert people into prospects, and then into paying customers. How do I do that with my business in insurance? What do I need to do on Facebook? What do I need to do on my website? What do I need to do on YouTube? It became about that, and so I switched gears mentally and went from this person who was just a content creator into more of a video marketer. Trying to understand not just the tactics, but really trying to understand human beings and what makes them do stuff, especially in insurance. I'm not selling timeshares in Bora Bora... I'm selling life insurance, all kinds of insurance, stuff that nobody wants to talk about, so it became my mission to learn how I actually get them to give me their money for an insurance policy. I had to figure that out. A lot of scars. A lot of trials. A lot of success, but a lot of things that people don't see that were complete duds."*

Now, I know Nick really well at this point. We have only hung out a few times, but we have video calls all the time to discuss strategies and tactics that we use in our own businesses. It's really cool to see the impact that video has had not only in this friendship, but in my friendships with a lot of the marketers around the world that have become very close friends. I feel as if we haven't really understood the power of video to replace in-person communication until recently. (We'll go over a list of ways you can use video in your agency right away later in this chapter).

When I started using video more in our content, and in our advertising for ourselves and for clients, I felt like I needed all this crazy gear. I bought a DSLR (Short for Digital Single-Lens Reflex, a standard digital camera anymore), a $1,500 DJI Mavic Pro Platinum Drone, two Go Pro action cams with the accessory kids and carrying case... Before I knew it, I was carrying around a bunch of gear on my back, and in the end I still ended up using my iPhone camera (which ironically was everything I needed to begin with).

Nick: *"Just look at the stuff that you watch online. How often do you see Steven Spielberg putting stuff on your timeline? You just don't. You know, I love that stuff and I have that stuff, but I have it because I'm a hobbyist and an enthusiast. I like gadgets, but do I need that to create content? Absolutely not. You don't need any of that. Focus on a $20 lapel mic off Amazon, get yourself a little bit of good lighting if you can, and just focus on the message. Focus on the framework, the script. Focus on how you're going to hook someone's attention. Focus on the value that you're going to give them and what you're going to tell them to get them to make a simple decision. The camera that you have on your iPhone is better than most cameras that you would buy in the store anyways. I think people use that as a crutch to be honest with you. I think they use it as "I can't make video because I don't have this or that."*

As he stated, there are a few critical things that you need to get people to watch your video content (for organic or paid traffic on any platform):

1. You need clean audio. This is really important. People can get passed less-than-good video, a lot of people watch video without actually "watching" the video anyways. But people will not stay tuned if the audio is bad. Invest a little money in a lapel microphone, as Nick said - $20 on Amazon should do.

2. Good lighting goes a long way. The biggest influence to most videos as far as how good they look is the lighting. If you have great lighting, you can play with your environment to get great video. If you have bad lighting, it really limits how you can use your video.

3. A camera. Any camera will do.

As long as you have the above equipment, you literally have everything you need to get started building video content. If you compare the modern iPhone to the camera standard in 2012, the basic technology now is probably superior.

Nick: *"Oh yeah, the iPhone 7+ will shoot 4k at 120 frames per second. There's DSLR cameras on the market that sell for thousands of dollars that don't do that stuff. So, just focus on the message. The machines are cool, all of that stuff is great, but if you prioritize the message over the machine... Just imperfect, fast action will get you a* *whole lot farther than thinking "I have to have this, that and the other". Because nobody really cares."*

IF I WERE YOU: In regards to any content that you have made or will make in the future, it's just about getting out there and getting it done. So often, people don't give themselves permission to be less than perfect as if any version of failure is final. Making content for your brand is the same as building a muscle. It's not always comfortable, but consistency will get you where you need to go. The only way to grow is to do it over and over.

*   **Nick:** *"I've even felt this way about advertising that I've done, and I can understand it. Especially if you're newer in your agency, I get it. You're not just sitting there writing off six-figure checks for stuff, I understand. And so every dollar is precious, every dollar counts. I totally get it. But when I advertise, I've had campaigns, and you probably have felt this way too [speaking to Preston], they've completely flopped. I will have spent $500 on a campaign on a weekend and not got anything out of it from a lead standpoint. However, if I flip my mentality to think 'Yes, I didn't get a lead, but actually what I got out of that was ad intelligence to know what's not working so that I can prevent myself from having a higher cost maybe down the road, or putting this in another strategy.' It's all in how you look at it. You have to look at it as if you are either winning or you are learning, and what you learned is going to allow you to win down the road. I understand the economics of it, but if you're in this for the long haul, if you're in this to have a sustainable process*

and way of attracting business to yourself... You just have to look at it as a learning experience."

Once you make a few videos and release them to the world to see, you start to realize that you're a human, just like the humans that are watching you... and it's just a camera, and you're just shooting video communicating with the world. You'll start to see the growth within yourself. It's pretty common not to be comfortable on camera, I still experience that. I could go a month or more without being on a Facebook Live video, and then when I finally make one I feel a sense of overwhelm until I am actually on again.

Nick: *"We have a guy in our program that said to me on a call, 'Nick, being on camera scares me to death. I'm not comfortable on camera. I don't know what to say, I don't know what to do.' So, I told him, 'Don't worry, we're going to help you. As much access as you'll give me is as much help as I will try to give you.' And he did his thing, he was just trying to bring brand awareness to himself and some local businesses... just as a value play because now when the camera goes off he's like 'By the way, I own an insurance agency', and that gives him new open doors. He went from being scared to death on camera to hosting his own Facebook show. It's really cool to see, this is for anybody who will just implement. Ideas are garbage, execution is what makes the money, and if you will execute and don't care about all of that mental crap... that's how you make money. That's how you get results."*

Implementing Video into Your Agency:

Now that you know video isn't nearly the demon we make it out to be in our minds, and that your phone camera is plenty sufficient to record every piece of content you could need, let's look at where we can utilize video within your agency:

1. Communication with your prospects/customers: Video proposals (see Part 2 of this book where we talk with Grant Botma about the power of video proposals), video voicemails, really anything prospect/client interfacing. You can use this on claims handling, or at renewal, this saves all of those office appointments and allows you to keep the personal touch without the need for both parties to set an hour aside (plus drive time).

2. Improving your website experience: A welcome video would go a long ways, you can use video to explain your quoting process, or what makes your agency unique and better than all of the competition. Be bold when using video to describe yourself and your agency, generally people will believe what they hear – so give them the best experience up front in video and back it up with how you deliver that service.

3. All email outreach to clients from welcoming them to the agency, to service or billing assistance, or policy

changes, cross-sell opportunities, renewals, all the way to trying to win them back after you lose their business. Video will allow people to connect with a human much more than text in an email.

4. Introduce yourself to new potential referral partners as a way to connect with them. If you show someone that you spent enough time to learn about them and that you made a message via video just for them, and that you want to connect and learn more about them and see where you might be able to help their businesses grow... That goes a long way.

5. Advertising! Facebook, YouTube, Instagram, any platform really... Even Google is prioritizing video into their algorithm to factor that into how you rank on their platform.

6. Supporting your blog articles. If you are blogging, and you have video content to support the blog and the headline of each are the same, that will improve your ranking on Google.

7. Video testimonials are huge: People love seeing that other people have already done what they're about to do, they especially love it when they see that it was a great experience. The most social proof that you can gather like testimonials, the stronger your case will be when they compare you to the competition.

Nick: *"I'm biased, but I think you have to do both. You have to do Facebook and you have to do YouTube... I mean, you don't have to do anything, but it's really in your best interest to do it. These are the two platforms that our customers and people in general use the most. They're either on Facebook, or they're on YouTube. So, I'm of the opinion 'Why don't I just haunt them everywhere that they go?' And I'll use Facebook ads to drive traffic to a page, and then I'll retarget them on YouTube and on Facebook. So wherever they go, they're seeing me."*

What Nick is talking about is a strategy that we use for agents called **Omnipresence**, which we discussed in the previous chapter. The beautiful part of marketing on multiple platforms and watching our prospects in Facebook, YouTube, Google, Instagram and the other platforms is that they might opt-in, they may not... Regardless, if they engage with or view your content you have the ability to follow them on these platforms and remind them of what's important.

While a lot of people ask whether they should be doing Facebook or YouTube, the truth is that as much as they are contenders in the advertising arena and as organizations in general, they also play very well together when you have them connected. Plus, this gives you flexibility. As all of these platforms have the potential to get buggy, or are subject to change, having that flexibility in your marketing will make sure that regardless of what happens with one platform, you have other irons in the fire.

Become the Celebrity

If you take this chapter in and really implement what we are talking about here, you're going to separate yourself from the market very quickly. Consistently getting the message out about what you do and why you are special and unique and can solve your prospects problems will automatically put you at the top of their list because you'll be one of the only people confident to be loud enough to rise above the standard noise of competition. You have to have some identity there, because there is heavy consolidation going on in the insurance industry like never before. But as I have always said, "Where there is chaos, there is opportunity". And the more context you add to you videos and other content, the more you give your prospects to grab onto during that ride.

Nick: "With that said, I do think that there's no better time to be in this industry than right now. It's not going to be any easier than it is right now today to move from the generalist on the pyramid to that authority, that expert, in whatever you're doing. The ability to take your phone out, send a message, and do that consistently, and have people actually take you serious, who knows how long that trains going to run... So you need to get in while the getting is good, and you need to establish and position yourself for the future of our industry. Let's call it what it is. There's going to be carnage and there's going to be people who don't do that. They're going to get passed up from a growth standpoint to people who do."

A great example of this concept is the team at G&N Insurance in Boston, MA. I have had the benefit of becoming close industry friends with Zack and Matt (who are also in the last chapter of the book where we discuss successful company culture), and they have done an incredible job of establishing themselves in the industry as an authority-gone-celebrity. They're taken it to the next level these last few years and hired a videographer to follow them around. This has made for a really strong content marketing strategy that helped them become well-known in the industry fairly quickly. Let's take a look at how the Pyramid of Power (created by Dan Kennedy) works:

So, you can see, at the bottom of this pyramid is the generalist. At the top is the celebrity. It's a simple concept to understand, think about doctors. Who makes more money, the doctor working at the ER clinic, or the Brain Surgeon? The specialist. So going from the generalist to the specialist is the first step. Then you need to leverage social proof (like testimonials) and a content strategy to communicate why you are the BEST specialist, when you do this enough you will become the authority. Then, when you continue to develop this presence, you meet enough people and your message gets out far enough, you evolve to become the celebrity. This is what you can actually watch happen in hindsight if you go through G&N content, which is really cool to see.

Nick: "If you look at how they became this household name in our space, they got on video. They told stories, they were consistently doing it. And because they were consistently doing it in a way that nobody else had done it in our space it built instant credibility, instant authority, instant everything to where now, I love them. I'm glad they did it because I wouldn't have known who they were in Massachusetts if they hadn't done this."

Being committed to good content with video, pictures, text, anything really... staying in front of your people builds relationships. Just like any other relationship in your life, the more time that you invest into it will generally create a stronger bond. G&N showed up, they formed a lot of friendships with other awesome people, and they connected with more clients and referral partners. It's a brilliant but simple strategy that anyone can execute on. Like the rest of this, the long play is almost always the right play. Consistent imperfect action wins.

Nick: *"The days of the early adopter are probably coming to an end or gone. Really, I think it's getting to the point where it's not just video, it's a lot of these things. You're either doing these things, or you're not doing these things and you're not as successful. It's no longer a luxury, it's almost a requirement that you are using video and these other tools. You need to be on social media, you need to be running paid traffic and you need to have an organic strategy. These things aren't optional anymore. We have to have these things."*

Which is hard to do, even as somebody who does this on a regular basis, doing all of the marketing that I am doing for ourselves and our clients, it's hard for me to do the other elements of the business. So, I'll be the first to give a verbal hug and say that while it is hard, it's going to be okay... It has to be done, and if you don't have the time, then you need to find somebody who can effectively help you. If you don't have time to manage your books, you hire a bookkeeper. Your marketing is no less of an important function of your business.

It's important to learn the most relevant platforms for your business first, and build a foundation of mastery there. That way you can build off of this as you grow and everything you learn going forward will make more sense with time because you always have your central understanding. The concepts in this book will definitely help you implement tactics and strategies on the various platforms as you will understand some of the underlying "Why" as to the outcome, but it's still in your best interest to learn more about Facebook as a platform, and YouTube as these are where your prospects and clients spend a lot of their day.

IF I WERE YOU: Find a mentor in the Facebook space, and in the YouTube space and learn from each of them how to be better positioned organically and with paid traffic. It's important that you have multiple sources of information so that you can integrate it all together. Different experiences from marketers will help you learn different techniques to get the results that you are looking for. This as much art as it is science, so by investing in coaching from multiple sources – you are amplifying your chances of success.

CHAPTER REVIEW: Decide which platforms you want to invest time and money in to and start executing. Don't worry about how clean it is, imperfect action will make you way more money. Also, with video you just need good audio, decent lighting and your cell phone camera. Keep it simple and take action.

UP NEXT: Now that you are starting to put together the pieces of your digital marketing plan, we're going to take a deep dive into how you can set up a winning strategy with your website so that when you run all of this marketing and start sending new prospects to it, they are more likely to convert into raving fans.

CHAPTER 4

The Relevant Agent
with Chris Langille

As our industry continues to evolve, it's important that we harness the power of the internet to the highest of our capabilities. In a world where people use apps on their phone to have drivers pick them up, find a partner by swiping right, or have food delivered from their favorite restaurant – we need to recognize and leverage the trend of human attention that is increasingly going toward the internet, specifically on mobile devices. People want to have access to knowledge immediately, there is a strong trend of consumers going where their instant gratification can be quenched. They want their questions answered, they want to feel protected, they want to know that they are getting the help that they want, when they want it.

At this point, an effective website is non-negotiable. The impact that it has on your brand is paramount to being seen in the digital age. It is where people can fact check that you are real, learn what you are about and how you can help them, maybe even feel like they can connect with you as a person. The availability that your website can create for your brand to connect with your consumers is incredible. In this chapter, we are joined by the best in this space, Chris Langille of Advisor Evolved.

Chris: *"It's interesting to see. Insurance consumers act when they feel pain. For instance, when their rate goes up. Or when they have a bad experience with their broker/agent/company/claim. Those are the times they're out looking around for a better solution. When they come to your website, it needs to help them in that moment. Keep in mind, at this point they are most likely not in the greatest mood, so you want to show them social proof [like testimonials]. You want to show them content that humanizes your brand and your agency. I see so many agency websites that are using stock art, stock photos. Not only does it look super cheesy, it looks like any other website out there. Really, your website is a branding tool, a marketing tool, a customer service tool, and a retargeting tool. There's so many things that a site can do. And if you think about it, a lot of business owners are paying $3,000 to maybe $10,000 a month for their physical office space, and they may or may not be meeting with clients in their office. But they're often completely undervaluing their website which is a 24/7/365 tool that is significantly less expensive than the lease that they're paying for their office."*

Aside from the obvious advantages of a strong website allowing potential buyers to get to you as easily as possible, there are many other benefits. A huge one being that when your website is done well, it helps convey who you are and what you stand for to the clients. You're not just selling insurance, people can get that anywhere now. The need for an insurance agent that is not unique in how they communicate with their current and future clients will continue to fade in the rise of direct to consumer models.

Chris: *"Branding has seemed to be a challenge in our space. But it doesn't have to be. Getting a new logo design is really not that expensive, but it impacts your website experience as well. It creates brand recognition, and when people see a good-looking logo over and over, they tend to be more likely to convert when called to action. When you have brand recognition like that, the leads will come. People don't know about GEICO or Progressive because of their blog. They know about them because they have built a brand through advertising... Think about their offer, they understand their customer base. A lot of agencies don't want to sell on price, but they offer nothing else to the consumer."*

This is an important observation, because I believe that every agent has a unique offer, but we fail to communicate it. We all sell insurance policies. We all help file claims and be there when shit hits the fan for a client. We all help make policy changes and explain coverage. But HOW are we doing those things? What is special about how we do that? What else are we doing that most people aren't, or at least that most people aren't openly communicating? Sometimes just breaking down every step of your process to provide the best service to the client, and itemizing all of the things you do to provide a top-level experience for them, helps you identify what you should be communicating to them as your unique offer. When I consult people, I often find that when we do a little digging of what the agent does to help the client, there is almost always a unique offer in there somewhere... But because we are in the trenches doing it every day, to us it's normal, so we stop communicating it. That's where we go wrong.

Chris: *"In this situation, understanding who your customer is and what your offer is to them, then driving the right type of traffic and having the right type of brand... that all goes into having success online. There are very few agencies that are checking off all of those boxes. I preach to my clients that these nuggets of advice might be tough love, but I want my client to win. If I say it's best to get a new logo, or change the images on your home page, it's because I see that you are missing on some potential conversion optimization or that your page isn't successfully trying to convey the message to the audience that you are asking it to."*

Now that we've identified that the primary role of your website is to provide brand continuity and be the bridge between your offer and your consumer, let's dive into the basic needs for your website:

1. Define who your client is. Who do you truly enjoy working with? Identify who you want to work with so

you can build the messaging to resonate with them. Dig deeper than "Good credit, owns home and 2 cars". What does their life look like? Do they share an affinity with you?

2.   Evaluate if your branding is in integrity with your ideal client. Does the logo have the colors and vibe that will resonate with your consumers? For instance, if you are targeting baby boomers, a hot pink logo might not be ideal. Does the website and content that you create reflect the type of information that your ideal client would want? If these answers aren't a resounding "YES", then you need to make a change.

3.   Start building assets that are in integrity with your ideal client. For example: Social posts, video content, brand assets, images, etc. If you have really poor images, or the file sizes are too small – it will distort on the website making it look unappealing and unprofessional. If you are looking to rebuild your website, it may be in your best interest to hire a professional photographer and videographer to film you and your staff, and the things that make you unique. This will add an element of professionalism to the experience, while allowing the consumer to connect with you as humans. At its core, your website is a framework for your content.

4.   Plan out your site structure. What do you want the client to see and experience? We figured out who

your client is, what would that individual want to see? What do they need to see that's going to make them feel comfortable to trust you and give you their business? This is a great opportunity to leverage social proof like video testimonials of happy clients. It goes a long way to show that clients are in fact having a great experience with you and it's not just hype.

Simple Yet Powerful

A great strategy to see if your website is conveying the message to your audience that you want it to convey, is called the **5 Second Usability Test.** It's a very simple yet effective way to see how effective your website is. Here's how you do it:

1. Find 5 people who have not seen your website and don't know your company or what it does
2. Have them view your website home page for 5 seconds, then pull it away.
3. Ask them what services or products do you sell?
4. Ask them what value you provide to your clients?

If these answers aren't clear or easy to articulate, then you need simplify your site. Let's break down one of the longest standing marketing concepts still in use today called the **AIDA** model, which stands for Awareness, Interest, Desire, and Action. This will help you understand a simple way to make sure that your viewers are seeing what you need them to see in order to make a purchase decision with you. You can communicate these concepts from top to bottom on your website on your homepage. We will use the website for Thrivesure Insurance below as an example of this through every stage:

Awareness: Where your prospects journey begins. Usually people at this stage have low commitment and are looking for value, clarity or assurance of your services. If you can't easily express your offer and the solution it provides to their pain, they will not be interested.

To be able to capture their attention at this stage, keep things simple. Try not to emphasize everything on your page because it confuses what the user needs to do. Your Call To Action (CTA) should be the only thing that is asked of them (and it's best to only have one CTA at a time), make sure that any messaging they are having at this stage points to the CTA. Also, if it doesn't immediately add value that will direct them towards the CTA, consider removing it. Especially in the insurance vertical, it's very easy to over explain. Keep headlines simple. Make sure that the CTA is easy to understand, like a button that says, "Click To Get Your Personal Protection Plan".

Interest: The consumer is now in-between Awareness and Desire, but still closer to Awareness as they aren't super committed yet. Since Interest is a self-selected thing, you can't really sway people to have a general interest. People who are visiting your website are generally doing it because they, at some level, have interest. It's hard to get people interested, but through a clean website we can take the interested parties and get them to take action.

It's best in this phase to give the consumer options so that they can self-identify with your services. A page that is aimed more towards people who are showing interest will have a few options to click, but not too many. We want to give them context without giving up clarity here. Now that they can specify their needs more, their interest can increase. A simple example of this with an insurance policy would be "good, better and best" in regards to coverage options, which allows them to choose the right fit for themselves.

Desire: This is when the consumer is starting to develop some commitment to your services and will start to invest time into the process. One of the most critical things at this point is to communicate safety and trust within your brand. Social proof like Testimonials is a great idea here.

Some tips here are to help provide information that the customer might need to choose you over the competition. What makes you better? Are your rates better? Do you have a specialty that better serves them and you're more familiar with? You can communicate this first person, or more effectively through third-party testimonials.

Action: If your presentation was strong at the Desire stage, this should be relatively easy for them to want to purchase from you. Reaffirm here with emotional triggers, what the benefits will be to their family when they have this policy in place. It can be as simple as "Click Here To Save Money" or "Click Here For Better Rates", or even deeper emotional triggers such as "Click Here To Protect Your Family's Future".

In the action phase, you are most likely getting them into a form or a survey. This is how you can obtain quote requests from your website. It's important to remember that a longer form will usually mean a higher level of intent (or commitment) from the consumer, but sometimes a simple Name, Email and Phone Number will do. Get what you need, but trim the informational fat. You don't want the prospect to feel like they're doing homework either. With that said, if you do have a longer survey, you want to make sure to ask one question at a time, rather than asking all 15 questions at the same time in your survey form.

Get A Quote

What Type Of Quote Can We Provide For You?*

◯ Auto Insurance   ◯ Home Insurance

SUBMIT

Every piece of content on your site adds up to the overall experience of the user. It would be wise to find ways to communicate that you have a unique service at any stage that it makes sense. Commodities are based on an extrinsic value system that is determined by the market. A consultative business is based on an intrinsic value system defined by the perceived value from the client.

Remember: People buy on emotions, and they justify with logic. Cater to this even in the simple messaging, and you will win your traffic over.

Whether you are investing in SEO, or Google Ads, or Facebook Ads, or YouTube Ads, or creating Organic content for your social media, it all has to point back to somewhere. If you spend any amount of time and money on advertising and marketing, but once the traffic gets to your website they leave without taking action – then it was incredibly wasteful. Every investment you make in your business is Gas, but your brand is the Car. This goes back to your offer and making it stand out. Every chapter in this book covers a component of your offer as an insurance professional. Even your website impacts the service to your customers.

Chris: *"The companies that are the most successful, whether you sell insurance or other stuff, are the ones that are really good at branding. Getting you to know their brand. Like GEICO for instance, I use them as an example because a lot of agents hate on GEICO. But if you look at GEICO's brand strategy, they barely even talk about insurance anymore. Their commercials are pure comedy.*

We want our audience to laugh. We want them to be entertained, and we want them to associate our brand in their mind with happiness and laughter. There's a lot of ways to sell insurance. You can sell it on fear, greed or you can be funny. They have taken that route."

Lean on Your Resources

When you are preparing your website build, there are multiple resources that you can go to for the assets that you will need to convey your message. For a new logo, you can go to fiverr.com, upwork.com or vectorstock.com. We had our agency logo designed on designcontest.com which was actually really cool. For less than $400 we had over 300 graphic designers worldwide competing to create the logo that we loved the most. There ended up being over 1000 variations that were created for our logo at Friends With Benefits Insurance Agency because we were really involved in the process and wanted the perfect logo. We ended up finding the right fit there. If you want a video banner or a whiteboard video created for your agency, fiverr.com is a great resource to go to for these types of one-off things.

It also helps to get content from in and outside of the office. Making this a part of your culture creates inclusiveness with your team, it goes beyond your website. It allows your team to bond and connect as individuals. Take candid photos of team members and yourself in the office, or maybe at an event away from the office. While talking with

Chris about this, he mentioned that one of his clients did a team building exercise in an escape room and they had a photographer there to capture the experience and share it with their clients. They used those pictures to add character to their about page with funny dialogue to support the pictures.

IF I WERE YOU: Make it messy. Get your hands dirty by working with some professionals to create the different media you need for your website. It might involve some of your time on the front-end, but once you have those assets created you own them, and it will add a more personal connection with your viewers. Always strive to make it messy, because messy means you did it... It is much better than staying in the stagnant land of perfect planning where execution never happens.

Chris: "One of the things that we do for our clients to make it easier for them, is we integrate our sites into Instagram. This is one thing that we created to allow our clients to be able to humanize their website and their brand in general, and that means that we have their Instagram feed on their homepage of their site. We want the visitor to see that the agent is a real person, just like them. This also makes it really easy for our clients to have updated content without a ton of work. Just keep your Instagram up to date and your website will constantly evolve. The simple things add up."

As Chris would say, it's important to approach your website and web presence with a left and right brain mentality because it's an art as much as it is a science. Fancy doesn't always make money, but stable doesn't always convert either. It's important to have elements of both. I used to look at my website like a digital business card, or like a sign on the side of the road. In time, I learned that it's actually part of the driving experience for the consumer. If a website is done properly, it moves people. It doesn't just tell them where they're at.

Chris: *"There's a lot of important things that happen during a person's visit to your website. How early in the visit are they seeing social proof? What is your call to action? What is your brand? You have a very small window of opportunity, especially with people who aren't familiar with you. Less than 2% of cold traffic converts on the first visit, so how are we going to serve ads to the visitor after they leave to get them back. They are going to leave, that's just what people do. They're going to check out other stuff, but if you have a memorable brand and your website has a clear, concise call to action with social proof and human elements, they're going to come back and do business with you."*

It's important too that you jump into this with both feet. There's a certain amount of gas that something requires to take off. You can't "kind of" put content out there for SEO, you can't "kind of" invest in your Facebook Ads. Whatever it is that you're doing, you have to commit and do it.

CHAPTER REVIEW: Find out who your audience is. Identify your brand and how you're going to connect with your desired audience. Start putting assets together for the website that you want to have. Build the website (or hire someone you trust to build it). Build content for the website. Keep driving people to your website. If you aren't comfortable building this, reach out to a professional for help.

UP NEXT: Now that we've discussed having a strong website, we're going to discuss how to stay top of mind within your community through SEO techniques and strategies. Let's start driving organic traffic to that website of yours.

CHAPTER 5

Don't Let Them Forget You
with Rick Dugmore

In pursuit of market dominatio, or even just developing local brand awareness with your community – one of the topics that is worth spending time on is **Search Engine Optimization** (SEO). There have been many discussions about which is better between SEO or Facebook Ads, and the answer is the one that you do better and more consistently. They both have their place in your agency.

I am joined in this chapter by Rick Dugmore who is an SEO Specialist based out of California, and we're going to break down what SEO really is. By the end of this chapter, you should completely know what SEO can do for your agency and why you should be using it, and how to go about getting started.

But first, it's important to understand how search engines really work so that we can expand upon these concepts throughout the chapter.

The Basis of Search Engines

As a consumer, the internet and search engines have been an incredible resource. Humans have never had more access to information than they do today, and it's because of this technology that we were able to do away with our encyclopedias. Search engines really have two main functions:

1. Crawling the internet for information that may be relevant to viewers and indexing that content for future viewing. Every web page, PDF, JPG or other file is part of this. You can imagine, that's a near endless amount of data, and that's why having content is not enough anymore. Your content must have context with your audience.

2. To provide the most relevant answers to user questions based on the user's keyword searches taking into account the pages that they have crawled and indexed.

To explain this as simply as possible, search engines use algorithms that find the content that has the highest relevance based on keywords and how similar the content is to the search inquiry. The results are then sorted based on the quality or popularity of that information.

If you haven't been proactively doing content marketing, you might be asking, what does this have to do with my agency? Insurance is no different than any other industry that has been compressed or consolidated in the rise of internet usage. Look at what Amazon has done to big box stores and malls. Plenty of disruption is going to occur within the Insurance industry because of the internet and it's really important to leverage search engines as a tool to be able to get in front of people that are asking questions. Questions that you could potentially answer and gain that consumer as a future client. People used to say that the internet was a fad, it couldn't possibly exist for long... Now there's a dystopian joke on the internet that goes, "We don't say 'be right back' anymore, because we don't leave. We live here now." People are using the internet at increasing rates with every day that passes, and people are searching for what they want. There is so much opportunity for you to grow your business here.

Rick: *"It's about leveraging tools. If you think about it, Facebook doesn't really own any of this content. They just use content that was voluntarily given to them, and make it more searchable, and now they're able to sell advertising space to advertisers. Google's the same way. Amazon was the same when they started. Ebay's the same way. Basically, everything was provided to them by us. In my business, I leverage Google. You [Preston] leverage Facebook and other avenues* *of marketing. People just need to be where their customers are hanging out now, and they're hanging out on the internet. And when they're searching for information on anything insurance related, that's something that you could be answering for them to get them onto your website. You used to run an ad in the phone book, or a print ad, and it would get delivered to their door or in the mail. Now you're creating content like an article or webpage that answers their question at the exact time they ask it."*

How to Start Using This Tool

Our primary objective is to rank as high as possible, preferably in the top three results, for the best possible keywords that people search for. But how exactly do we do this?

Google says the best thing to do is, "Make pages primarily for users, not for search engines."

So, I think the answer is pretty clear that the next is to find out what people are searching for that you want to compete on. For instance, let's assume that your goal is to focus on selling more Homeowners Insurance, you would start to reverse engineer what the users would be searching for that corresponds with that topic. If you want to rank higher, search for those keywords for your local market. The smaller your area you are trying to dominate, the less competition you have.

Rick: *"Say you want to sell home insurance in Sacramento. What I like to do is called indirect result blogging. Basically, you blog about the city, just to bring local relevance to your website. I have clients that have posts about local fishing, or best restaurants in town. We do this to bring local traffic in, so Google sees local IP traffic coming into your website, seeking these random topics. It makes sense though, because you're in the local area. You should be creating value in your community. I do this as an indirect way of ranking my sales pages, because now Google see's that I'm getting more local traffic from my competitor and I'm offering more value to my local area. I might already have relevant content, but now I have popular content and now I start to rank higher on Google. As an added tip, you can feature other local businesses as well on your blog to bring local relevance. When I do this for a client, I email the local business and say 'Hey, we featured you.' Then they end up sending me their website traffic, or sharing my stories on their social media, which helps generate more popularity for our website which ranks us even higher."*

IF I WERE YOU: Use Google to find out what people are searching for, so you know what to build your content (ie blogs) around. Write down a few questions you think people might have around a topic, say "Home Insurance" and then start searching. Google will prefill the more searched topics. For instance, as I am writing this book if I type in "What does my homeowners insurance", it gives me the following:

G   what does my homeowners insurance cover   I

Q   what does my homeowners insurance cover - Google Search

Q   what does my homeowners insurance cover **state farm**

Q   what does my homeowners insurance cover **usaa**

Q   **what should my homeowners insurance cover**

Q   **what does my aaa homeowners insurance cover**

Q   **what does my homeowners insurance policy cover**

This is more of a national topic, and you would be competing with a lot of people for clients that you might not even have state licenses to sell insurance to. So it might be better to start searching for things more local to you like the following:

G   best sacramento insurance   I

Q   best sacramento insurance - Google Search

Q   **best car insurance sacramento**

Q   **best homeowners insurance sacramento**

Q   **best health insurance sacramento**

Q   **golden best insurance sacramento**

Q   **best renters insurance sacramento**

Rick: *"Also, when you do a search for a question, Google has a feature called the question knowledge graph. Type in your main question you get about home insurance, and scroll down on Google a*

little bit, you'll see this tool. You'll see other questions popping up that you can click on. Those are the most commonly asked questions. You could literally create a whole article with all of these questions as subheaders and categories within one article, all about the questions that people are asking. It can be fun, because when you click on one, a new set pops up. So essentially you can get an infinite number of questions that are being asked and create your article about the ones that you find important."

This is a great strategy to help you come up with the blog articles that you want to make to generate inbound calls to your agency.

A Realistic View

On average, Google has ten positions that you can rank for on the first page of results for any given search. Those results are ordered by **rank**. The closer to the top spot you are, the higher the rank.

The top few positions generally get the most traffic coming through for searches, which makes sense since the people asking these questions don't have a need to look much further if the information provided on the first few results was sufficient. So in turn, the better your content, the more relevant and popular it becomes. Then it ranks higher, and higher ranks get more traffic. Well written blog posts and web pages have the ability to generate a lot of traffic which can turn into a great revenue source for your agency.

Generating results can take time though, because Google has to index your content and then it has to rise the ranks. If it is great content that answers the requested information, it will become more popular and rank faster. If it is not received as well, then it could take longer.

SEO is not immediate, nor is it ever complete. It will take time for you to rank, and you have to keep creating new content to ensure that you stay in a good position. A lot of agents that I speak with don't understand the commitment these things can take, and I get it – it's a lot of information for an Insurance specialist to take it when they already have a full time job.

Rick: "I would expect results to start happening from SEO within six to nine months, and potentially up to a year because Insurance is a really competitive niche. But there are ways to enhance that for your agency."

Which leads us to our next section...

Short-Tail vs Long-Tail Keywords

Depending on the keywords that you are looking to compete on, you will have a completely different experience. For instance, there are vastly different results for the keyword "Insurance" than there are "Used Honda Insurance in Tacoma Washington". Way more LARGE companies are competing for the Short-Tail keywords, because it's easy to build and there's a lot of traffic that goes to it. Which also makes sense for a company that is in all 50 states, but that isn't the case for most agencies. So let's dive into the difference between the two types of keywords:

Short-Tail: These are 3 words or less. The above term "Insurance" would be an example of this. Or more realistically "California Home Insurance" would be a short-tail keyword.

Long-Tail: These are more than 3 words. These keywords will usually have far less search traffic than their short-tail cousin, but they also have less competition over them, and they are more specific so you can make high quality content specifically for these people. An example would be "Home Insurance for California with Solar Panels."

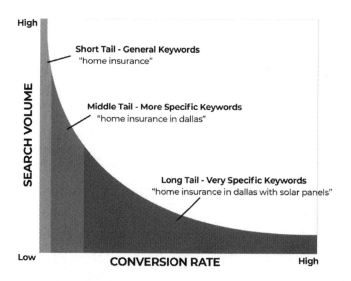

Generally, as keywords get longer you will see the search traffic reduce, but most companies see a significant increase in conversion with the long-tail type traffic that exists there. Major companies like Allstate in the insurance world, they are doing national TV commercials and using billboards. They are advertising in as many places as they can, as well as investing in their SEO. For them though, it's much less about the Call-To-Action than it is about brand recognition. They want the constant exposure, where are we want to have the prospects convert into clients.

Rick: *"Often times, if I rank a client for 100 long-tail keywords, question-based stuff, and I help you dominate all of those low volume searches, they would add up to be equal to or potentially greater than the traffic you'd get from ranking for a short-tail keyword. So, you might not be ranking for 'Homeowners Insurance California', but you're ranking for 100 other things that gives you the same traffic volume. The quality of those searches are often much higher as well. That's where insurance agencies win in the SEO game."*

SHORT TAIL   VS   LONG TAIL

Short Tail	Volume/Competition/etc.	Long Tail
★ High	Volume	Low
High	Competition	Low ★
Low	Focus	High ★
High	Cost	Low ★
Low	Conversion Rate	High ★

IF I WERE YOU: Start with long-tail keywords and build your way up. This will help you start to get positive results faster, and you can start to build your ranking up over time. Then you'll have a stronger platform to play the shorter-tail keyword game.

A Golden Nugget

Rick: *"You can use a paid tool called ahrefs.com to gather keyword information. What I'll do is enter a website that I believe to have a lot of industry credibility or traffic, like Allstate for instance. Or maybe a competitor of yours who's getting a ton of traffic. I would enter their website into ahrefs.com and click on a button called "top pages", and I will see what pages on their website are getting the most traffic. I know their homepage is getting a ton of traffic, so I can't really do much there, same with their contact page. But then I will look for their top five blog articles, and I will see if I can write an article around that topic and make it better. Then I will grab the exact blog article URL, and then put that into ahrefs.com and grab all of the keywords that it's ranking for, and then I'll put that in a CSV file or an Excel File and just tell my writer I need to include these keywords or these topics, since I have this article, because I know that they're ranking for it and I want to steal their traffic."*

The Low Hanging Fruit

One of the most simple things you can do to effectively compete with SEO is by creating your Google My Business (GMB) listing. If you haven't already set up your Google page, you can create one and then Google will send you a postcard with a code on it. Once you enter that in it will verify your listing and that's how you start building your placement on the map within Google searches.

Rick: "You really want to have Google trust your website. By completing your GMB listing you're taking a huge step in that direction. When we onboard a new client, we make sure their website structure is dialed. We start out with the sales pages, each service, the homepage, the contact page, things like that. We take care of the blogging on a monthly basis. But the first month, I always set up the GMB listing. That's going to bring you the most leads of people who want your help, without having to wait months for it to take effect."

A Google My Business listing is free to set up. Go to business.google.com and type in your address, and claim your listing. Once your listing is verified, it's important to start filling out the information that they're asking you for and optimizing it. This includes your business description, hours of operation, photos of your business, etc.

Having your GMB listing also allows for you to start getting reviews on Google as well. Keyword relevance even impacts the reviews that clients leave for you. If a current client raves about how good your service was in helping them with their Home Insurance for example, when someone locally searches for Home Insurance, that review will be prioritized because it is regarding what the search was about. So even reviews are impacted by keyword relevancy.

Rick: "*Reviews are huge. They're one of the number-one factors of ranking a Google listing.*"

It's really beneficial as well to upload a variety of photos to your listing. Interior and exterior photos, your team members, working with clients, etc. You can also set the radius for the area that you serve, which can grow as you build credibility and trust with Google. You can even create a Google website where you can write out sales copy and publish it to get more traffic for Local searches.

IF I WERE YOU: Start making posts onto your GMB listing. Posts that you might be making on Facebook or Instagram for instance, post those as well on your Google My Business listing. They allow you to make posts directly in the GMB dashboard, so people can see those posts in search engines and that will help boost your traffic and get more inbound calls or website views.

Rick: "*If you get a review on Facebook or Google, take a screenshot of your review and post the screenshot in your GMB listing images. Then copy and paste the review URL and say, 'We appreciate your review.' This will allow for you to repurpose your reviews so that more people will see your social proof. Also, I would do the services post. I would talk about your services and have strong Call-To-Actions in there with your phone number and "call now" buttons. If you're not posting to your GMB like you would Facebook,*" *you're behind the curve. Your competitors will take traffic from you if you aren't proactive."*

It's also important to apply the correct categories to your business within your GMB listing. This can also determine whether you keep or lose traffic. Do a Google search for industry keywords for the city that you're in. Say it's "Homeowners Insurance Seattle". See what category they're using on the map, it can change depending on your search keywords used. You can rank differently for different categories.

Rick: *"After you set up your GMB listing, you want to keep it as simple as possible so I would outsource this next task. You should create what are called citation directory listings for your business. I would recommend going to brightlocal.com, enter in your company information and then create an account with them. Order the top 50 citation directory listings for your business. Each industry has a set of top citations you should have, and they'll create these for you. The goal is to create industry-specific and major citations for your company with a consistent name/address/phone number across the web. Once you do that, Google reads all of these citations and starts to correlate that with your GMB listing, which builds trust with your listing. Just make sure that all of your information that you're putting to these citations is exactly the same to your GMB listing. Whether it's a pound sign (#) or a Suite (Ste), or it it's a Lane (Or Ln), make sure it's spelled exactly how Google My Business lists it."*

Once you have built out a strong presence within your GMB listing, it's important to keep maintaining it but you can also move onto other parts of your SEO strategy as well (like your website and blog articles, for instance). Google is expanding their tools available to you as the business owner because they want traffic to stay on Google properties for as long as possible. So they will make sure to treat you well for leveraging all of the tools that they create. There are plenty more things that you can learn about SEO, and that will continue to evolve with time – but once you understand these core components of how to leverage search traffic on Google, you will start to have a very healthy source of inbound calls and revenue.

CHAPTER REVIEW: First step is to build out your Google My Business Listing and optimize it with all of the content that you can. You will also want to create blog posts, articles and web pages that provide content/answers around people's search queries. Doing this consistently will make a big impact, especially with long-tail keywords.

UP NEXT: With a firm understanding of marketing, your web presence and SEO you are well equipped to dive into the discussion about how to use your presence to build referral relationships. The next chapter is all about how to establish yourself as the idea referral partner for other industries.

CHAPTER 6

Building Your Ecosystem
with McBilly Sy

Being in the Insurance industry can be a very isolated experience. So many people hold their agency practices close to their chest, and form habits of distancing themselves from potential allies.

For instance, an independent agent might distance themselves from other independent agents due to seeing them as competition, or from captive agents because they might think they have nothing in common. Not every agency has the same appetite so we aren't all competing at such a fierce level as we act sometimes. The most successful agents that I know are ones who have built bridges to other people, in and outside of the insurance industry.

I know from our experience, when I started to meet with other people in the marketing world and in the insurance world, it had a direct correlation to the increase in our bank account. I went from being the smartest guy in the room (which doesn't mean much when you're the only one in the room), to an eager student of the industry. It goes deeper than that though – we started to build a network of people that would refer us business, and vice versa.

I'm not talking like a network meeting type thing where you meet once a week, I'm talking about genuine relationships with other agents, Loan Officers, Real Estate Agents, CPAs, Lawyers, Inspectors, etc. It was about building my community around me and becoming the architect for this Ecosystem.

If you're tired of taking in cookies and muffins to people that aren't working with you, then this will transform how you build your network of referral partners. In this chapter I am joined by McBilly Sy, my business partner, who runs our mortgage marketing division and back-end systems to break down how you can become the architect of your own Ecosystem.

Breaking Down the Ecosystem

When we started testing out our system, we wanted to make that we were developing the most efficient method to build referral relationships that exist within the insurance vertical. Through testing multiple different relationships, we experienced a need to make the relationships about volume. Many people work towards transactional business, where one action can get you one sale. This wasn't the approach that we wanted to take, and so through trial and error we build the Ecosystem around a very simple framework. Insurance Agent -> Loan Officer (LO) -> Real Estate Agent (RE)

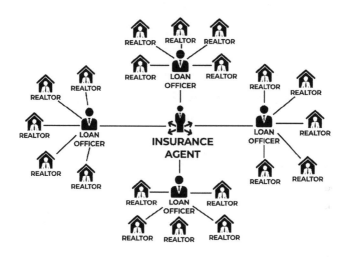

Our Ecosystem technique is about establishing a dominant relationship base with Loan Officers. The higher the level of authority that they have at their branch or company, the better the relationship can be for your agency. We will go over how to attract them later in this chapter, and the different experiences that you will encounter so that you can be prepared, but for now – understand that your most effective contact will be with Loan Officers. Once we have established a relationship with a Mortgage Professional, we help them deepen their relationship with their realtor referral partners so they are able to expand their offering as well. The beauty of this system is that if you have done it correctly, you set your mortgage professionals up to be the face of the operation so that they get the credit with the realtors, but you're the one moving the levers. Which means that all business funnels back to you, and you're positioned in a way where it's advantageous for the Loan Officer to have you in their inner circle.

McBilly: *"If you focus on the high hanging fruits, the things that most people aren't willing to reach for, that's when you start to see long term success. Relationships are becoming more of a necessity every day. Instead of just going after individual consumers, which is fine to do, you add in the high-hanging fruit of referral relationships for long term revenue. It takes a little bit more time in the beginning, but if you're able to cultivate relationships as you help your referral partners with their business and maybe even take it a step further to connect with new Real Estate agents to further their relationships, you become the architect and those relationships will literally create the whole Ecosystem for you. This will generate new business with every passing day. It's such a huge opportunity right now."*

For the purpose of this book, we will break down how to attract the Loan Officers to work with so that you can start building your Ecosystem. If you want to expand to be able to help your mortgage partners connect with real estate professionals, go to digitalnativesacademy.com to speak with us about additional strategies that we can teach you to build deeper layers in your Ecosystem.

So how do you source the ideal referral partner?

Partner Attraction Methods

Before we talk about **how** to attract partners, let's talk about **what** to look for. It's important to understand what you're looking for in a referral partner so that you get real results. There are plenty of insurance agents across the nation that try to entertain Loan Officers that don't produce, and get frustrated because they don't reciprocate your attention or your efforts. If you're entertaining a low volume LO, they don't usually have much to send back to you in the first place.

Things to look for when you are deciding on whether someone is potentially a good fit:

1. They produce, as mentioned above. We don't want you spending time where there is no benefit for your labor. Invest in people who have things to invest back in you.

2. They have industry tenure. This isn't a full requirement, but traditionally an LO that has survived a few years in their industry is much more familiar with their products and how to take care of the client, and more importantly you can leverage their organic network that they've been building on for years.

3. They respect your processes. It's important that you are able to do business on your terms. If you are investing into a referral relationship, you shouldn't

have to be doing dummy quotes because they are giving you limited information, or them trying to distance you from the relationship until the loan closes.

4. They work WITH you. Find someone who wants to build synergy with you and work together to give the best service possible to the prospects. You should be involved in the process and building the relationship with the prospects as well, working WITH the LO to give a quality experience to the new home buyer.

Finding Your Partners

Running a marketing agency that heavily serves the mortgage industry nationwide gives us incredible insight into the lives of these Loan Officers. We generated tens of thousands of homebuyer leads last year and we will do more this year, which allows us to see what Loan Officers are doing to have success on a personal level and state by state, because every market can vary – especially when the markets consolidate due to rate changes like we're currently experiencing.

Now, I wouldn't recommend doing this without prior discussion and a sense of true need from the LO, but we have seen that the insurance agents that are able to realize the deeper desires and needs of their referral partners; Those who can find a desire to increase production volume and help build prospecting and sales systems, and then generate long form homebuyer leads for their partners have the most success in building long term relationships.

Seeing these trends while consulting with various insurance agencies nationwide on this process, we've realized that there are multiple different ways that you can source referral partners to work with, so that you are finding the best fit for your agency. The partners that are willing to work in a way that benefits you both mutually. Here are a few resources to search through:

1. Premier Lenders on Zillow and Redfin. Look in your local area for the Mortgage professionals that are at the top of the list. These people are spending money to be there, which means that they understand the need to invest in themselves, and they will be more likely to appreciate you investing in them too.

2. Google search the following: Mortgage, **Your City**, **Your State.** You'll get local professionals, start with the people who have the most Google reviews on their Google My Business listing, and work your way down.

3. Search on Facebook for Mortgage, and then go to "Pages", and then search in the "Local Business or Place" category. You will find local Mortgage professionals and you can sort them by likes and reviews. Both are indicators that they are active

which means that they could be potentially great people to network with.

4. Scotsmans Guide: This is a list of mortgage professionals, and companies by production. It does not list them all, but it does have a good amount. You could definitely find at least a few people in your state to work with from this list.

5. Your current sphere of influence. This can be easy depending on the relationships that you already have. If you have realtor connections or mortgage connections, follow it to see where it could go.

These should be more than enough resources for you to go to in your search for the right referral partners. Keep in mind, it only takes a few solid mortgage professionals to start adding a good amount of revenue to your agency. Finding the right referral partners is the key to success.

As for the "How" in regards to connecting with Loan Officers: When you meet with LOs, spend time genuinely trying to learn about them and their business. Ask them about the systems that they have and where they are experiencing pain, discomfort or feel that it "could be better". Sometimes they need more leads, sometimes they want nothing other than for you to genuinely do what's right for their client. What's important here is that you don't assume their needs. From our studies, we have seen that most insurance agents approach Loan Officers trying to offer "Fast binders, great service and the lowest rates", which we should all be offering, that is the standard. Some try to send leads without knowing whether or not the LO has a pipeline or leadflow issue. This doesn't always win the relationship and sometimes it can be viewed as unwelcomed. Simply asking questions to provoke deeper conversation around their potential problems in business can give you massive insight into the value that you can provide for mortgage professionals.

McBilly: *"Set your partners up for success, which will eventually set you up for success."*

IF I WERE YOU: Find 3 Loan Officers/Branch Managers that you want to approach to form a referral relationship. It's important to start small and give them what you can, and then build on that. There's no need to try to get 10 partners until you have a system down.

Once you find the people that you would like to meet with to see if working together would be a good move, now you need to approach them. I personally prefer to do some research on their social presence, their reviews, if they have video content or blog content that I can read, or anything else they may have that is unique. This information will give you insight into how creative they are in attracting customers organically, but also it gives you a foundation for reaching out to them in conversation.

This is more of a "dangled carrot" approach that I use, but you can send an email like the following to get the conversation rolling (feel free to make it more "you" by changing whatever fits your style of communication more:

Hey *NAME*, I was doing research on Zillow when I came across your account, and to be blunt... I want to work with you...

I saw that you do a good job for your people from the reviews on Zillow - and that's really important to me...

and I want to make an offer to you better than just cookies and cards or coffee dates like other insurance agents...

I am looking for a mortgage professional I can build a relationship with around clients of mine and prospects that I am generating with my agency. I have a marketing system SPECIFICALLY for mortgage leads because I believe in investing in my partners.

My goal is to help you grow your business, build trust and be able to help your clients with their home insurance as well...

Yes, we have fast response to binder requests, good service and awesome coverage/rates/claims service... but at the end of the day, I am willing to invest money into this relationship if it's a good fit because I believe that's good business and you have to water a plant to watch it grow...

If you are open to discussing a potential referral relationship that we can develop, let me know and we can meet and discuss what I am doing that will help you make more money...

Talk to you soon.

YOUR NAME

Now let's dive into how to establish the relationship on a healthy foundation.

Qualifying Your Partners

If you've done everything up to this point, you should already have some emails back from LOs to get together. The goal is to learn about them and see if they are a good fit for your business just as much as it is to see if you're able to provide them some form of value as well. Learning how to say "No" is just as important as your desire to say "Yes" to a new relationship. First off, how are you truly able to add value to a mortgage professional's business? What is "value" anyways?

If you were to ask someone you met for the first time, "How can I help you?" they won't be prepared to give you a good answer because most people don't hope that they walk into someone who can solve their problems. So here are a few sample questions that my friend and fellow agent, Matt Naimoli (more from Matt in Part 2 of this book) recommends you ask to get them talking about their business in a way that will dig up potential areas of opportunity for you to provide value back to them:

- What would you do less of if you could?
- What would you do more of if you could?
- What do you love most about your job?
- What do you hate most about your job?

- What challenges did you experience this year that you wish you could overcome?

After you have learned about them, you should have an idea of where they are at. The conversation should be a mutually engaging conversation, if it's not and you're constantly leading the conversation you should either evaluate your approach with the LO or question if it's a good fit. If they are engaging back and asking how they can help you too, or asking questions about your business, that's a good sign. That's a relationship you should foster.

There is no "one size fits all" solution to what your referral partners will need. The best thing you can do is listen to them and learn about their needs from the conversation, once that is done these things work themselves out organically.

Investing in Your Partners

If your agency is in a situation where you are wanting to financially invest in your referral partners in generating leads and helping fill their pipelines, then you have multiple options. You can learn this from a marketing agency, or have it built for you by a marketing agency to manage yourself, you can request more information about available solutions like this at digitalnativesacademy.com.

I would definitely recommend for the agent in their first two years to proceed with caution on spending money to build the pipeline for your LOs. Referral relationships aren't generally an immediate return on your money, and if you can't afford to invest into something for a few months before you see it return a profit – than my advice is to find more organic ways to feed your referral relationships. While investing in a relationship financially is a pretty huge sign of good faith, I would only recommend it when you have predictable revenue coming in from renewals.

It's important to remember that most people that are looking to buy a house aren't going to do it sooner than 90 days out. Some will, but it's about setting proper expectations as well. Your loan officer may or may not close loans within the first month, they may not close loans within the first 90 days of you running a system like this for you... There are a lot of variables outside of your control here, but you should be good to go as long as you communicate that these are exclusively generated long form leads, and they understand that these convert at roughly 5% just like most top tier lead sources. This is a numbers game, and they have to have effective sales systems. If they don't, then buying leads might not be a good solution.

McBilly: *"If you hear people say something like "Well I convert at 60%, so 5-10% is really low", they are referring to referral business, which they should be converting closer to 90%+ if we're all being honest. That is traditionally the statement from someone who hasn't worked a lead system, consider it a potential red flag on whether of not you want to work with that person."*

To expand on that, when you are doing lead distribution for your referral partners, what we have had massive success with is providing an automated 3-channel follow up to help support them in their prospecting. This is when you use automated texts, emails and voicemails to contact the leads so that the LO doesn't have to. This allows for the leads to still be worked, but you aren't adding much work to their day. Then, they handle the incoming responses. If you give a LO 50 leads a month, and they have to call every one manually to try to contact the leads, then often times they will say that the quality is bad because no one is picking up... But when you automate the follow-up and send texts, emails and voicemails on their behalf – you save the LO a ton of time. Plus, this makes it so that your referral partner only has to work the leads that are responding to the automated follow-up so their job becomes easier. You will find that the more a Loan Officer has to do to convert a lead you provide them, the less attracted they are to working your system.

It's important to remember that you can give the same 100 leads to two different mortgage professionals and there's a high likelihood that one could say they "suck", and the other could be extremely grateful and make $10,000+ out of it. Mindset plays a huge role in this system.

IF I WERE YOU: Find a way to remove all the barriers that your referral partner is experiencing in their prospecting. By automating the texts, emails and voicemails, you achieve a good amount of this. You can also get the leads that you generate to schedule appointments with your referral partners so that they have scheduled calls which increases quality of the leads. You can even create a testimonial page for your referral partner after the leads opt-in to edify your LO and help the prospect see them as the expert.

Managing the Relationship

The important part of having a strong referral relationship is a dynamic of reciprocity and gratitude. If you have sourced out ways that you can help, even if that's as simple as being there when they need you as your availability may be their true desire, then do your best to honor that if it's a relationship that you want to foster. Proactively seek ways to fulfill that, and make sure to communicate your needs as well. If you have an internal procedure that you like to do when getting referrals, allow your referral partners to know that so they have the opportunity to respect it.

An open line of communication goes a long way as well, make sure to prioritize time to nurturing the relationship just like you do to creating the relationship. Just like anything else, a plant that isn't water will eventually die.

Referral relationships are a high-hanging fruit that a lot of people aren't willing to reach for because it takes time to build the relationships, and you have to invest your focus into them. They are also very rewarding because of that. A well-managed relationship is the backbone of many of the most successful agencies in the nation.

McBilly: *"Your time is worth much more. Instead of doing the data entry, policy management or answering billing questions, you can focus on building and maintaining these relationships that are bringing in business, while hiring someone to do the $15/hour work for you. You can now give yourself a massive promotion."*

Know When to Cut Ties

If you are making sure that your actions are in line with your desires, and you maintain that integrity in your relationships, you will know if you need to cut ties or not. If your referral partner is not respecting your business procedures or asking you to do things that make your job more difficult because that's how they do business, and they expect you to be the only one to be willing to meet in the middle, that's a tell-tale sign of a toxic relationship.

If you feel disrespected, the first step is to communicate it from a place of seeking resolution for the problem. Try to avoid anger. If you still feel disrespected after you have openly communicated your disapproval of the relationship dynamic, the third step is to evaluate if it's time to cut ties. The third and final step is to remember that there are a ton of loan officers in the world and a lot of them are great human beings. Some of them are bound to be your kind of people, so keep searching and don't settle.

CHAPTER REVIEW: If you are looking for a waterfall of "wins", start building your referral network. This allows you to go from transactional business to relationship business so you can scale your sales up without spending a ton more time prospecting.

UP NEXT: Part 2 of the book is all related to Time. We will be going over different topics to help you be more efficient and have more available time to sell, or be with your family, or be in the world living your passions.

PART 2
<u>TIME</u>

"I don't have enough time. I am being pulled too many directions Someone or something is stealing my time. Whether you complain that you are overworked and overextended, or you believe that other people, obligations, or competing loyalties are forcing you to postpone or cancel your own aspirations or dreams, you're basically saying one thing. You are inefficient. Yes, it's your fault. It's bullshit and you can change that."

-Jon Taffer

"I have not failed. I've just found 10,000 ways that won't work."

-Thomas Edison

CHAPTER 7

An Hour Saved, An Hour Gained
with Grant Botma

When looking through your agency to find ways to be more profitable, selling more policies isn't the only solution. It's a great solution, but as you continue to grow, inefficient processes and wasteful time management can become parasitic to your ability to reach the levels you want to achieve. In this chapter, we're going to talk about a simple and actionable way to reclaim your time hour by hour. I'm excited to be joined by Grant Botma of Stewardship Insurance and Neoteric Agent.

Industry Compression

It's become more necessary than ever to have a close eye on profitability as the insurance industry gets exposed to all of the change that is happening. Between increased competition and the emergence of Insuretech companies, rising rates causing decreased retention, and companies lowering commission rates – it's a tough time to be an insurance agent. For the professional willing to adapt and grow though, there has also never been more potential than there is today within this industry.

Grant: "In insurance, our margins are getting squeezed and they've been getting squeezed for a really long time. We have carriers that are quite literally on the fly changing how much they're paying us in commission. They are requiring us to re-sign new contracts with them, which is crazy. Because of the competitiveness in the market, premiums aren't rising as quick as the rate of inflation in some markets, so the costs are going up, but our income is going down. This is a problem. I knew I had to either get out of insurance, or get better at it. And just from a business perspective, if costs are going up and income is going down, I have to find a way to make income go up or make expenses go down."

Need for Efficiency

Grant: "I focused on expenses, and the number one expense to any business is employees. What they're costing you, the issues they may be causing you or just payroll in general. So I said, "Okay, if I'm going to grow I need to make that payroll expense as low as possible and to do that I have to be able to do more, handle more customers, handle more policies, do more service work and write more new business with less staff." That was it. That was when I realized I had to do this or my agency wouldn't be as profitable as I need it to be."

When evaluating your business to find areas of opportunity to reduce wasteful spending, consider a potentially new way of thinking: Wasteful doesn't have to be unproductive anymore. Wasteful is LESS productive than it could be. Reframing the way you view your expense of time and money will allow you to see the other opportunities that exist around you. You might find that you have buried a sales star in your agency with service work for years, but you wouldn't know that they've never had a time to shine because, "They never had time" to sell.

The agent who wins is not the agent who has the bigger book of business, or how much premium you have – there are a lot of factors into where you might be profitable, and where you might be bleeding heavily even when it sounded good on paper.

Grant: *"I knew that I had to be able to run my business in a way that my employees can handle a very large number of customers and a very large number of new business policies compared to the average. That was my focus. I went into a deep dive study and focused a ton of daily effort in determining how much time my staff was spending on different things. Where are their bottlenecks for customers? As part of that I found not only a bottleneck for my staff, but I also found a bottleneck for my customers. That bottleneck was the time that it was taking us to put a proposal together, and more* *importantly the time it was taking consumers to respond to those proposals."*

This used to be a really big issue for me. I remember when I would send these biblical length insurance proposal emails. Which was overwhelming for the prospects, I'm sure. I would always quote with a "Good/Better/Best" format to give them options knowing that they would often choose the middle option, plus it was better to give three product options than two general options of **yes** or **no**. Even then, conversion was lower than it should have been and I had spent way more time on it. This was the best case scenario too. I've always disliked the in-office appointment, but sometimes people would prefer to do that compared to the emails I would send. Every time someone came into my office, I would lose between 30 to 90 minutes. It was incredibly wasteful.

Grant: "Exactly. You didn't want to type those emails, but we're still doing it and this is what most people do. It takes us so long to do them, and the reality is most of the data in there, most of the information in that is similar for every client. You're typing the same things over and over. But here's the real problem, it was taking customers a long time to respond, so I studied why. Why are customers taking forever to respond? Not only did I survey my current client base, I studied society and pretty much became an anthropologist and behavioral scientist. I listened to a lot of podcasts, read a lot of books from Harvard professors and such, and it came down to this quite simply.. People don't read emails. I looked in the mirror and asked myself, "If I see an email, and it's several paragraphs long, what do I do?" I punt it. I might have to read it, but I don't want to read it right now, and so I wait until later. Then I say to myself, I'll get to it tonight. Then I'll open it later that night and after a long day I don't want to deal with it right then, and so I keep punting it. That's what our clients are doing, they're seeing these, as you said, biblical length emails with attachments of stuff that they don't understand, and they're punting it, and they keep punting it."

I'm sure you can even think of a time like this for your agency where you were literally saving the client hundreds, maybe even thousands of dollars a year, and they still wouldn't respond. Where most agents go from there, is to try to craft better emails. Maybe if you become more wordy they'll respond. Or maybe if you talk about more technical policy detail, they'll recognize you as the professional.

In the end, it turns out that everyone on both sides of the transaction was actually yearning for simplicity and didn't know how to communicate that.

The New Opportunity

Grant: "I wanted to change that, I wanted to template the process of creating proposals and more importantly, I wanted to create a proposal in a way that consumers actually enjoy. Here's the big paradigm shift for me, here's the thing that I decided I wasn't going to do that every business does. I was actually going to meet the *customer where they're at. I was done trying to do things my way. I was done doing things the way that every other insurance agency did it before me, even though they might have been successful. I was going to genuinely determine my target market, how do they think, and I'm going to create a communication style and process that is in line with what they're already doing in their life and in line with what they're already doing in their mind. I was going to meet the customer where they're at. It catapulted us, it helped us skyrocket to new levels, which was great."*

When you have staff, as experienced agents know, you have to make sure that you're working hard to ensure that everybody eats. If you care about your staff, this is important to you. A lot of people in this industry put pressure on expenses, but it's a more traditional approach. If margins run low, they cut expenses. They don't refine them. The beauty of this perspective on efficiency and expenses is that when an agent practices this – they turn their liabilities into assets. Sometimes expenses don't need to be cut, they need to be refined into something better. This allows your staff to be more productive, and purpose becomes a beautiful consequence in your teams lives at work, as people are allowed to challenge their potential again instead of being stuck in the land of "well this is how it's always been done".

Grant: "Anyone can cut an expense, but what we need to do as business owners is make the most out of our expenses. Payroll and overhead are expenses that are a requirement for business, so how do

I make the most of that? The same is true for advertising. Advertising is a requirement, I have to budget for that. How can I make sure that the money I'm spending for advertising is the most efficient? That's what I did with this expense on overhead with employees. I have to pay employees; how do I get the most out of that expense?"

Enter the Video Proposal Movement

Imagine having your clients receive a video recording of you explaining the policy you are proposing, presenting your product to the consumer in a way that they can understand, and show to their spouse and quickly buy insurance from you. This is the power of video proposals. The idea here is that you want it to be quick and easy by creating proposals from ready-made templates to save time. With this, almost everything you send to the client is pre-made, except for the short video you can create to make it personalized.

Grant saw this blaring need in our industry and he raced to provide an ideal solution which does exactly these things, called Neoteric Agent.

Here's what is important to know about using video proposals with your clients:

1. It allows them to connect with you in the most human form. As we continue to integrate video into our client's experience, it acts as a very direct replacement for in-person meetings. People get to experience not only the words you're saying, but they

see your body language and tonality. They get to see how passionate you are, and that you care. They see that you are invested in protecting them. (Remember, people buy on emotion and justify with logic)

2. It opens up a lot of time that you would waste sending long emails where you are sending a similar version of the same thing to different people. The amount of wasted time in a day when you are doing that is parasitic to your productivity.

3. No more 30-90 minute appointments in the office. This has been huge for efficiency for us, because we are able to serve 6-20 people via video in the same amount of time we would have one in office appointment because...

4. It only takes 5 minutes to completely record a proposal and send it.

5. You will notice that your clients are watching these videos during their free time which is normally after the traditional 9-5 structure. This means that you are getting work done even when you're not working. That's the start of really cool things.

My personal favorite thing about sending video proposals is that I'm able to communicate the solutions I provide to the problems that the client has in a way that makes sense to them, and then they hand the phone to their spouse and let their spouse watch it. This allows for me to properly explain our solutions to each member of the house so that they can make an educated decision to do business with me.

When you present via email, phone or in person, you are usually presenting to one person. This person probably has a third grade education level with their finances. You explain their options to them, which sounds good for now, but then they try to re-explain to their spouse what you said to them. The spouse ends up hearing this third-grade reiteration of what your proposal was and says, "Yeah that doesn't sound good", to which you are now getting ghosted by the client or told that they are going to "think about it". This happens too often even in the times that you are saving them money because you're communicating in a way that is least beneficial to the consumer.

IF I WERE YOU: While I believe that Neoteric Agent is totally affordable for all agencies, if you are in a really tough financial pinch you could start off with using Loom video recorder for free so that you can begin making positive changes in your agency. Go to useloom.com to learn more about it. It's totally free to download and after you record a video it gives a URL that you can send to the prospect to watch the video that you made for them. Either way, start using video proposals in your agency.

While using video proposals will streamline your quoting process, what is beautiful to watch is the rate at which clients will respond to resolve the quote request. The amount of chasing that the old model requires is intense, and it can often be weeks until a prospect spends the time that it takes them to open your email, completely read it, decide if they want to work with you and then respond. That's above and beyond the time it takes your staff to gather the data, do the quote, type the proposal and send the quote. This takes weeks down to days, allowing you to realize the commissions from your sales sooner, allowing you to reinvest in your lead sources more to create a positive feedback loop of success within your business.

Grant: "Quite simply, businesses don't exist without the ability to find needs and fill them. So if every day we as business owners don't have that mindset, we've failed. Find needs, and fill them. We need to find a way to do have that mindset and think that way every day and in every process possible, whether it's with our employees or our customers. So the need again was I was taking forever to type up this email, attach something and send it, so what can I do? Well I can template things, I can create a process that says, "Click this button, autofill this". Here's an example, for auto we quote 100/300 [liability], and 250/500 [comp/collision deductibles] often. So I wanted to create a template that said, "Hey here's a customer that wants 250/500, click this button, and have it even template down to the carrier's specific policy details and add-ons".

Keeping It Simple

It's about removing barriers and allowing the prospect to buy from us with as few effort requirements as possible. It's easy to assume if they don't buy from you that you didn't sell them on the value, but often times the value is more than coverage or price. For some it will be the simplicity for them, and the ease of access to you as the agent. Think of this, you create a proposal via video and have a link that you can share with them. You then text them this link so they can watch it. Compared to the 20-30% average open rate of email, 98% of text messages are read within 2 minutes, so there's the first barrier – gone. If you are partial to email, you can also email the same link to them to ensure that they receive and read it.

Once they receive that message and open the link, they'll go to your video. They click, you're there explaining the coverage to them. They don't even have to read. Second barrier removed.

Now they've seen you, they see that you are emotionally invested in protecting them because they're able to watch you explain the coverages in the way that an email or website can't. They also have the ability to hand the presentation to their spouse for them to view it which helps the spouse get good information, but it also frees the primary prospect from the burden of trying to explain concepts they may not understand. Barrier three is now gone.

Once they agree, or maybe they have questions, they just click a button on the proposal to let you know that they are ready or that they have questions. They don't have to call or type, it allows you to be able to reach out to them now without making them type out a response. Barrier four has been eliminated because we're not waiting on the prospect, which allows us to do our job much faster and efficiently instead of waiting on them to complete simple actions.

Grant: *"Here's what we find typically happens. We send the text message, they open it within five minutes because with Neoteric you can track when someone's viewed your proposal. Then we find that they view it again later that evening. So here's what I imagine happens: They're at work, they get the text and open it like, "oh cool". And then they get home and after they put the kids to bed because that's when you have time to do stuff as a parent, they click it again and the primary prospect probably tells their spouse, "Hey check this out". After they view it, "Wow, isn't that neat? Yeah, I understand it". Then later that evening we're getting notifications at oddball hours that say, "Hey look they've accepted your proposal, let's go!" So the process that we had when we would send email proposals out, the average time that it was taking people to respond and say "yes" to a proposal was almost 12 days. Now it's less than 24 hours and people are literally making purchase decisions within that first 24 hours because we met them where they're at. We're delivering the proposal to them in a way that they want on their mobile phone, in a text message. We're delivering it to them in a way that they understand in an infographic with a video."*

Most of the time, the insurance agent sending the proposal is far qualified to explain the quote, but when we face a lack of conversion, a lot of agents tend to default to information overload. That's not the solution. Sometimes, and this is one of those cases – less is more. Once we simplify the process for the prospect (and in turn for your team), everyone wins.

Grant: *"The cool about video is when you're first starting, you can record it. If you don't like it, re-record it. If you don't like that, re-record it. Eventually you have to just go with it, but to put it simply, here's three steps to succeed using video proposals. First, sign up for a free trial. Second, dive in and actually do it. Third, experience success with your customers and referrals."*

CHAPTER REVIEW: Educate and empower your clients in a way that meets them where they're at. Remove the barriers for the clients to buy through simplifying your proposal method. Take action, and start using video proposals so you can be selling more or spending time with people you love.

UP NEXT: We will discuss how to use the power of automation to run lean at your agency. Allowing your team to produce more and handle more service without the need to hire more people.

CHAPTER 8

The Agent Who Cloned Themselves
with Will Shaw

As I travel around the nation meeting new insurance agents, I often ask, "What do you think would help you be more successful in business?" The response is often a variation of, "If I was able to duplicate myself". It's a fair request, and now more than ever before, this has become a very realistic thing to achieve.

In this chapter, I am joined by one of the most knowledgeable automation specialists in the insurance industry, Will Shaw of Marketing Connected We're discussing the topic of automation and how it can make a massive impact on how much your agency is able to comfortably get done.

This is still a relatively new topic to the insurance industry, and there are a limited amount of people that know a lot about or are heavily using automation within their agency. Outside of that, most agents don't know what they don't know, and so they continue to operate the same way that they have been for years. Even with that, those same agents struggle through manual tasks, while prospects and clients continue to fall between the cracks when agents exceed their production bandwidth. Let's talk about what automation is, as well as what it isn't.

What is Automation?

Automation is a series of pre-defined events or tasks that happen when a specific event occurs. For instance: A quote request comes in, and an email automatically goes out to that prospect letting them know you're working on it. This is a simple example of an automation. Essentially, you are removing the need for manual labor on tasks that are happening over and over within your agency. Systems can do all kinds of things to help you and the client have the best and easiest experience possible. A few of the most common automations are the sending of emails, texts, phone calls or voicemails when certain events happen.

Will: *"If you think about it in the simplest terms, most prospects take on average four emails to convert into a client, and on average each email takes roughly 15 minutes to create and send. Even if it's a* *short email, because you have to mentally stop what you are doing, go read their email, think about what you're going to write, write it, maybe get distracted while you're writing it, and then finally send it out. So if you think about automating just those four emails, that's one extra hour that you have in your life from EVERY client that you take on."*

That's a small example, but even that becomes a massive reclamation of your time at scale. When you start adding all of these simple automated tasks up, you have potentially hundreds if not thousands of hours' worth of labor that you could reclaim and either spend with people you love, or selling to new clients. Either way, it's critical that you leverage this tool to your advantage in order to have a highly profitable agency and a better quality of life.

What isn't Automation?

Automation is not designed to replace you as the agent, or even your staff. This isn't an industry disruption that is going to put (the good) agents out of their careers... While some people believe that automation is scary or intimidating because it could create some dystopian insurance industry terminator-esque future, the most successful agencies that I know using automation use it so that they are able to reach and help more people. Not just more people, but to do a better job of helping them. But if you take a close look at their agencies, they are still VERY human-centric.

It's like building a house and going, "OH! I don't want to buy a hammer... I already have a contractor". Well, give the contractor the hammer. You don't choose the contractor OR the hammer, right? Having the tool and the manpower allows for you to do awesome things.

Outreach Communication Types

There are various tools that you can use in an automated fashion to get more done in every moment. **Emails** are usually the most common for people to start off with because it's something that you are most likely already doing manually and familiar with sending them. Next would be **text messages**. Not every agent uses text messaging with their clients, but I would highly advise you to do so since so many people communicate via text now. After that you have what is called a **ringless voicemail** or a **voicemail drop**. These are really helpful for getting a message out to prospects in bulk through what is called a broadcast, where you send the same message to multiple people. This is useful in an event like a catastrophic claim to let every client know via voicemail what your contact information is just in case they lose computer access. Even **direct mail** can be tied into automation now, which can be an effective method of using direct mail if you use it to support your other attempts to reach a prospect.

Normally, we will use these different communication methods combined in a sequence over a certain period of time, as there are two primary factors that influence contact rate. The first is consistency. Often a prospect or client is not readily available the first day that they become a lead or make a request of your agency. So it is best to keep the sequence ongoing over the course of multiple days so that you get in front of them at a day and time they are available to speak with you. The second is preferred communication style. I have seen through testing with tens of thousands of leads how important communicating with your prospects and clients through these various communication types is. Some people will only text you, some will only call, and some will only email. If someone will only text, and you will only email – it's as if you are speaking different languages and the transaction may never take place.

Will: *"If you're struggling to figure out what to put in your emails to start creating some of your automations, here's a good example for you to use. We've tested with hundreds of thousands of emails, and the number one performing email I've ever personally been involved in uses the subject line, "Sorry for my last email", or "The last email was a mistake", or "Whoops, I messed up". Something to the extent of human error because it intrigues the reader to open as it triggers their core desire to know information that others may not. Automating human error can even work beautifully."*

Focusing on the Relationship

Let's talk about how automation helps you expand on the relationship and deepen the connection to your prospects and clients. Most agents, especially in their earlier years are spending most of their time working IN their business. You are on the phone, you are doing the data entry and getting quotes prepared, you are selling the insurance, you are maintaining the relationship and handling billing issues and policy endorsements, you are handling claims conversations. There is a lot that you are doing. The amount of time that you have to spend to do a great job of all of those tasks for some of your clients, takes away your available time and focus from the rest of your clients. Eventually, you either have VIP clients that get most of your time, or you get spread too thin and everyone suffers. Automation allows you to pass some of these tasks off to your system, so that you can focus on working ON the business. This helps your clients because you have oversight and can ensure they have a great experience instead of trying to be the one responsible for creating that great experience in every moment.

A concept from the e-Myth that is very applicable to this situation, is that you want to take yourself out of the technician role so that you can be either the manager role or the visionary. And whichever you can't be, you need to hire out. There really isn't a way to automate the visionary, and you are limited on how you can automate the management (although certain functions can certainly be automated).

The Big Difference

Once you start to reclaim your time through automation, you are no longer chasing prospects. Now you have automated the outreach so the system does that. So now you are able to handle more sales calls because you are making less cold calls.

Here's a tangible example: 2 different agents generate 100 leads through Facebook. Agent 1 has no automation in place and Agent 2 has automations in place throughout their sales processes.

Agent 1:

When those 100 leads come in, Agent 1 is spending a lot of time prospecting with what feels like little return on his time invested. Best case scenario is Agent 1 is doing their job properly, they will make at least 100 Calls day 1.

Let's say that they get in touch with 10 of them via phone call and 5 are wanting a quote, now Agent 1 has to decide whether they quote the 5 households now and let the other 90 available leads go stale, or do I keep making prospect calls and risk letting my 5 quoting opportunities go stale?

They continue to play this game for a few days, but they end up not making nearly the amount of phone calls they need to effectively start conversation with those leads, and at a certain point they are most likely going to stop being intentional about their sales process.

They start slipping. They stop leaving voicemails, they stop emailing, they stop texting, and eventually they stop calling. Agent 1 feels like generating leads doesn't work well and doesn't equate to sales. They may break even year 1, and hopefully they have decent service and retention systems so that they keep those households to year 2 so they make a profit. Out of 100 leads, this agent may sell 10 households.

After the initial phase, best case scenario is this agent will enter these leads into an x-date list to call at a future time that, hopefully they will call.

Agent 2:

When those 100 leads come in, all agent 2 has to do is make 100 phone calls on day 1, and hang up... Because his system is automatically sending texts, emails and voicemails on his behalf.

Agent 2 finds time in the day to make 100 calls because it's all they have to do, so it's much easier for them to systematize. After 100 texts, emails, voicemails and calls have gone out for the first day, agent 2 finds themselves with about 15 conversations started for day 2.

On day two, agent 2 starts working the quotes for the first 15 conversations that were generated through his automated messages. Agent 2 has 5 good quoting opportunities, but he still has 85 phone calls to make. While he is doing all of this, his system is sending texts, emails and voicemails on his behalf, and these leads have also been scheduling appointments with agent 2 because he connected his calendar to his prospecting system to give the leads an opportunity to choose the best time for them. This will go on for the remainder of the automation sequence that agent 2 has created for these prospects.

Agent 2 will have communicated with roughly 50-60% of the leads minimum when they are done, if they have been calling while their system was sending texts, emails and voicemails. Out of 100 leads, this agent may sell 30+ households. After the initial phase, this agent has placed these prospects into a future effective campaign to remarket in 5-6 months (which most of this will be automated as well, freeing the agent of this responsibility).

You can see how agent 2 has a huge potential to generate much more revenue and be much more profitable than agent 1. They can also take the money from their successful campaigns and hire someone else to sell with them, essentially doubling their sales potential.

The smart agents will not only leverage this technology, but also realize the future revenue they can generate by growing with these systems. One of my biggest frustrations when I used to be a captive agent was when I was told, "You've gotta pound the phones" for personal lines business, or "You gotta pound the pavement and knock on doors" for commercial business. Nothing I did was directly measurable. Nothing I did was quantifiable at every point. I remember having 80+ hour weeks that I would work, and sometimes I would have something to show for it, and sometimes I didn't.

That's a really abusive place to be in your business, having to go home and you have to tell your family, "I have nothing this week…" You've been away from your children all week, away from your partner, you missed their game or recital, you'll never get that week back. That was the worst. I swore by my life that I would strive to never have those moments again, and that really started the journey of automation for me and our agency.

Now everything is 100% quantifiable at every point. If something isn't working, I can accurately diagnose where we are having issues.

Think about the 100 leads in the above example? If you were to call them, text them, email them and leave voicemails for each of them every day for 7 days, that's 2,800 outreach attempts… It's a task that you shouldn't give yourself. But if you automate the texts, emails and voicemails, you automate 75% of the work, and you only have to make 700 calls over a week's span. That becomes MUCH more manageable.

Will: *"The sooner you can get to a lead as well, the higher your chance of conversion. Imagine a lead coming in from Facebook. Within 90 seconds, they're getting a phone call. We have tools that allow for larger agencies to keep multiple agents in rotation in front of the leads so that the phones are always being answered and leads are always flowing in. The agents can dial out to four or five people at a time and whoever picks up, it will take that call and leave a voicemail for the others.*

IF I WERE YOU: Design your agency for consistency. If you have leads without automation, you are going to overwork yourself or underwork your prospects. If you have automation without leads, you've essentially built a house to remain vacant. Both marketing and automation work hand in hand to ensure that your agency has stable growth into the future.

Stages of Your Client Journey

There are an endless amount of possibilities as to how you can utilize automation within your agency, but I wanted to gather a few examples so that you could understand a few simple places you can start to implement these kinds of tools.

1. Prospecting
2. Quoting
3. Sales
4. Welcome to agency
5. Renewals
6. Referral Gathering
7. Obtaining Agency Reviews on Facebook and Google
8. X-Dates and Requoting Opportunities
9. Referral Relationships
10. Lead Sourcing

Depending on how your office is set up, there are a variety of different tools that you can use to support these automations.

One system that is awesome is the Lightspeed Voice VOIP phone system. On top of handling your agency phone lines, it also allows for all kinds of automations to be tied into the platform so that you can connect your office lines directly to everything else you are doing to communicate with your clients through their Follow-up Tool software. Makes for an incredibly easy entry into the world of automation.

Will: *"When planning out your client journey, you want to start at a high level, and then work down from there. If you look at an insurance lead, what is the overall journey? The lead comes in, you need to have a conversation with them to get their information. Then you need to go and do the research to find the best policy you can find for them, deliver that policy and they either accept or decline it. That's your most fundamental level of what's happening. Now, each of those stages, or those steps in the process, has a couple different things that could happen. Even if they move forward, or don't, more things can happen. But that's the high level overview. So now, when you start niche-ing down here, when a lead comes in, what's our first priority? Let's get them scheduled or get on a call with them. What are the best ways to do that? Sending them emails, text messages and dialing out to them. All of which we can do, basically, without you actually spending any time doing it."*

Once you have the prospect scheduled, you are going to go through the other phases of your sales process like data gathering and quoting, and then you will send your proposal or sell the policies in person, but even after that your job isn't done.

Will: *"Now that we have won the client, our job isn't done. Now what I want is for the client to start referring people to us, without our client having to pick up the phone, and take the time to ask them for it. This is one of the things we can do in the welcome sequence, welcome them to your agency family. Let them know what your team is about, let them know your dedication to helping them. This is where you start to build an emotional connection with the client and will start to trigger referral opportunities that yield results when you do ask for referrals through automation. You can automate birthday cards and thank you cards, and when renewals come you can not only discuss requoting them but potentially cross selling too."*

Cross-selling is a huge area of opportunity for a lot of agencies as they already have a relationship, so there is free money already in the agency ready to be grabbed with the right communication method, message and effort.

Will: *"I have conversations with agents all of the time, where 90% of their book is mono-line. It is so much easier to get money from someone who has already bought from you than it is from a stranger. Using automation in a situation like this can take the agency with 80-90% mono-line down to below 40% mono-line potentially in time. From there, it's about increasing coverage for clients and shifting that relationship to the next level."*

IF I WERE YOU: Be intentional with your clients. If you use a whiteboard and build out the current experience that your clients are having with your agency, and then find out where you would like to add or remove things, you will begin to visualize where you can be a better resource for them. That's the necessary first step to knowing what to automate.

Map out everything. What happens if you can't get a hold of them? What happens if you do get a hold of them, but they're not ready, or they're not qualified? What happens if they do move forward? What happens at each step that you currently have? It's important to keep your feet in the dirt and keep your head in the clouds. Meaning that you should have simple and practical things you execute on, but try to also find unique and new ways to serve your clients.

Superman to the Rescue

Most agents that learn about automation immediately dive into building out prospecting and sales sequences, which is a great place to start. But it doesn't stop there. There are plenty of ways that you can use automation to enhance your claims experience so that your clients feel supported when the bad moments in life happen.

An easy way to allow your clients to report a claim to you is through the use of a ticketing system like Fresh Desk or Zen Desk (or any other ticketing system), you can embed these systems into your website to create a claims portal where your clients can file their claims. You can then have that ticketing system connected to your automation platform to make sure that the prospect knows that we received their claim, as well as notifying you of the claim, and then adding reminders for you to report or process the claim to the carrier and stay in touch with the client.

Systems like this ensure that the job gets done and the client stays satisfied with the high level of communication which will solidify that relationship in a time of need. You can even set up tasks for a virtual assistant (we go over this much more in the next chapter) or a member of your staff reach out to your clients to ask if there is anything else that they need during this tough time. As you can see throughout the chapter, none of the automation was designed to replace the person, but rather to support them to allow them to achieve more in their daily lives.

Rallying the Troops

Some agencies struggle to get their staff on board with newer technology or systems. I sometimes hear, "My employees don't really care, they don't want to have or use these systems. I know that these would help but I can't get my employees to adopt these systems and it's hard to find good licensed staff." All of these things might be true, but if you put yourself if your team's shoes, they probably don't want to change because they have zero direction and their desire to invest into the business is low.

This happens in all industries, not just insurance. If you have zero direction, and you're just thrown into something and have to figure it out, you will look around and feel really lost. You don't know what is good or bad, a win or a loss, and so you settle. The beauty of automation is you help them get more done, so they can be more productive which will help everyone make more money. They will also have more purpose because they can make a positive impact on more lives. So hold firm on making these changes into the future, and lead from the front. If they see you using these systems and having success, and they know that it's expected of them as well, you'll learn real quick if your staff is REALLY on your team, or if they've just been comfortable with their paycheck. When you increase efficiencies in your business, the weaknesses expose themselves.

Stay in Your Zone of Genius

I want to reference a book called the Big Leap that helps you identify your skillsets by where they fit into one of four categories. When you are reviewing the topic of automation which can be quite an involved process, I want you to ask yourself the following questions:

1. Is this in my zone of incompetence? If automation is in your zone of incompetence, then hire it out immediately. Understand it enough to USE the technology, but don't waste time trying to build it when someone else could do a much better and faster job than you.

2. Is this in my zone of competence? If automation is in your zone of competence, and you kind of want to

figure it out – feel free to play around with it, but understand it would still most likely be in your interest just to hire a professional to do it, and you can consult with them on how to make improvements. You want to stay where you are worth the most money, and brings you the most happiness.

3. Is this in my zone of excellence? If you feel that automation is in your zone of excellence, then you probably experience joy from building automation sequences and using the platforms, it's probably not a horrible thing for you to be doing this. Make sure that you are finding where you can be most valuable, but this might not be a distance second place for you.

4. Is this in my zone of genius? If automation is in your zone of genius, then hire producers and CSRs to sell and serve your book of business and start building out an amazing series of automation sequences so that you can do what you love and build a self-lubricating machine of an agency.

Even I feel that automation is in my zone of excellence, I enjoy it and I can do it – I'm definitely not the worst at it, but I still feel that it isn't my gift to the world, so I usually hire it out to Will for him to build for me, and I act as a visionary for what I want to exist. In my down time, I will build sequences too, but I only do it when I have free time. So, find where this fits for you, and do what you need to do to implement automation into your agency, whether that is hiring it out or doing it yourself.

Will: *"Be great at what you're great at. Find somebody to help you take your business to the next level. If I'm talking advertising, I don't do my own advertising. You [Preston] do my advertising. I could do it, but that's not my native genius. I could go and build out every system, and be the tech behind everything. But that's why I have a team to help me build these things. Because really, my native genius is strategically implementing systems and processes to increase conversions at the same time. So as an insurance agent, if this isn't my primary skillset I would be asking who can help implement this for my business, so that I can be great at what I do, but become even better than I thought I could be."*

IF I WERE YOU: Time is money. If you aren't confident in your skills in automation, it can take a long time to learn. While there are a lot of resources available to get started in learning it, and I believe that you are fully capable to do so – you need to ask yourself if it's worth the time. If you can hire someone to build this out for you for a few thousand dollars, that is much cheaper long term than spending dozens and maybe hundreds of hours trying to figure it out yourself.

CHAPTER REVIEW: Using automation tools will allow for you to massively increase your productivity in almost every part of your business. More free time means more revenue generating potential, or more time doing what you love. There are many ways to use automation, and they don't have to be complicated.

UP NEXT: With your agency developing strong systems, we dive into how to leverage virtual assistants to outsource your more standard tasks to free your time up to focus on higher revenue generating tasks.

CHAPTER 9

Call in the Reinforcements
with Wess Anderson

If you have started at the beginning of this book and read through to this point, there has been a lot of mention about how technology within marketing and other components of your agency can help modernize you, and all of them have a very necessary place in the top performing agencies in the nation.

I'm excited to discuss how to we can not only leverage all of these amazing tools to help you be productive, but also how to utilize outsourced staffing to make your primary staff much more effective and efficient. I am joined in this chapter with Wessly Anderson of Agency VA, a virtual assistant firm that helps insurance agencies realize new levels of production with less work for their office staff.

While outsourcing has been happening for decades now, it's a concept that is just now starting to enter the insurance industry.

What is Outsourcing?

In simple form, outsourcing is the act of delegating a task to someone who is either more systemized to complete a certain kind of task (think accountant), or to someone who is more competitively priced due to currency exchange rates that work in your favor.

You'll recognize the act of outsourcing with most major companies if you were to call and speak with them. This includes companies in the tech sector, finances, credit card companies, phone companies, even major insurance companies. I remember when I was a captive agent, our company outsourced our underwriting support to an Indian call center.

Wessly: *"It's been happening for years. But we realized a need specifically for insurance agents, we know their pain points very well. We knew from our own experiences that we could successfully have virtual assistants fix these problems. It's more common than it is revolutionary at this point, but it's extremely fitting that insurance adopts a concept like outsourcing later than everybody else. It's been the biggest blessing for me in our agencies, is that fact that the industry generally moves slow because I move fast. It's super advantageous for me."*

I can appreciate the fact that the industry is antiquated in that fashion. I have always said, "Where there is chaos, there is opportunity". I think that we are now starting to seize a lot of this potential for ourselves in the industry and the people who adopt these concepts first will be on top over time.

My Own Experience

As an agent, I am inefficient at tasks like quoting. It's very necessary, but just like data entry it's a task that we get stuck in that detracts from our ability to be involved in the high revenue generating activities. When you evaluate the need for certain tasks, you have to ask yourself if you are more important and valuable in the role of sales or in the role of data entry? That's a simple example, but I realized that when I did an audit on the things I was spending time on within my agency, there was no way I was going to be capable of making the money I wanted to make with that structure. I was weighed down by work that wouldn't propel me there.

Letting Go of Resistance

I've heard some agents express fear that outsourcing their job could cause impending doom to their ability to run/own an agency. Or that somehow outsourcing tasks would be the first step towards a world where there is no job for them to be able to have. Newer ideas can be stressful, no one wants to be the first human who learned which berries were poisonous.

Wessly: *"I think the model behind it is met with fear because it's unknown and it's new within insurance. It's always a similar process when we see insurance agents start to implement virtual assistants. The magic happens when the agent realizes they've been paying someone $17 or more per hour to do a $10 per hour task, and it changes the way they look at their business and the value of their time."*

The reality is that if you think about it, you've been outsourcing for a long time. Do you do your own taxes? Do you change your own tires? Do you take your trash and recycling to the dump every week?

I'm sure you answered "No" to at least one of the above questions. We're going to dive in to the reasons why it's in your best interest to start treating the tasks you have at work just like changing your own tires.

Just like we discussed in the last chapter about automation, you want to think about the interactions that you have with your client. Where are we connecting with them? Simple moments like billing issues or adding a vehicle to their policy. Imagine having another person answer your phones that you don't have to pay $17 or more per hour, and they gather data, and then transfer a call to you if it's sales or handle it if it's service. Imagine being able to focus on just selling, if you could free your staff up from the burden of paperwork so they can experience the blessings of free time to sell. The potential for this to benefit your agency is really big. Let's touch on some examples of different processes or tasks that you can plug a virtual assistant into to free your time:

- **Every unlicensed task**: It's a pure waste of resources to have your licensed staff doing tasks that are not required to have an insurance license for.
- **Data Scraping/List Building**: An old school form of prospecting to gather contact information from a multitude of different sources. While it is tedious on the front-end, there is still a lot of benefit to doing this.
- **Answering your phones**: You could technically give your agency 24/7 call support by outsourcing your phones to a team of virtual assistants.
- **Data entry:** This is something all quotes require, and some interactions even require you to do this more than once. This task is definitely not worth what you are paying your local staff to work for you, but it still has to be done.
- **Cold calling businesses or lists:** Have a virtual assistant make the calls for you to set up your appointments from a list. A potentially high ROI scenario for your agency. An old-school tactic that can still have a lot of power.
- **Re-shopping clients at renewal for rate increases**: Very necessary for your retention, but once again, this is a very simple task that can be outsourced.
- **Policy endorsements**: Pretty straight forward, but a good example is adding or removing a car.

- **Sending emails to clients and carriers**: I treat my VAs just like a member of my local team. They get a company email and I inspire them to take control of their interactions with clients and carriers.
- **Educating you**: I will have my virtual assistants read a book that I want to read and then have a call with them where they give me their notes and we hold our own book club essentially. This inspires me to want to be involved because it's more like a group project now. So it's much more exciting than reading a book, but I am also training my team member while they are helping me grow.
- **Training us with technology**: You can use virtual assistants to learn a new technology so that they can come back to you and teach you how to implement it within your agency.
- **Birthday outreach**: You can have your VA send happy birthday messages to all of your friends on Facebook. These little acts consistently show that you care.
- **Gathering signatures**: If we aren't getting a client to return needed signatures for an application, we will have our virtual assistant do it for us so that we can continue moving forward while our VA spends the time to connect with a less available client.
- **Pulling and organizing statements**: Whether carrier reports or commission statements, you can have your VA help you avoid wasting time on any kind of report.

- **Personal needs**: You can have a VA that works like an executive assistant. They can book you date nights with your spouse, buy airline tickets for you, set doctors appointments up.
- **Technical editing**: You can have your VA transcribe audio or video, or even edit audio and video for you to use as content for your brand.
- **Maintaining your social profiles**: VAs are great at tasks like keeping your business pages up to date throughout the social atmosphere.

As you see, there are a TON of ways that you can leverage virtual assistants as an insurance agent, and there are many more that we still haven't listed. If you implement even 10% of the above listed things, your life would change drastically.

You're Over Qualified

Think about it, there are agents out there that have acronyms after their name like CIC that are doing policy endorsements. These people have extra education, they have studied hard to join a higher level or risk management knowledge, only to be stuck doing $10 an hour work?

Wessly: *"Every CIC person that's adding a car, I'm telling you right now, you're killing yourself. You should be doing other stuff. The virtual assistant coming in to help service clients frees that CIC's quality CSR or agency manager to be generating revenue for the* *agency instead of making a policy change. The number one area of improvement I feel to be service, and a very close runner-up is market acquisition. Agencies that are successful with lead systems of any sort, be it lead generation or referral partners, the successful agencies are the ones that have strong people with strong sales processes."*

IF I WERE YOU: Hire a virtual assistant for your agency. The paradigm shift that happens in successful agents is that they realize outsourcing allows them to maintain integrity between where they say that they want to be, and what they are doing to get there. You can't value your time at $500/hr and do $10/hr tasks, that will never be a winning equation.

Training Your Virtual Assistant

Say you hire a virtual assistant today to help you win back your time, you may find it daunting to train your new team member because most likely, you haven't gone through a process like this before.

The first thing that you want to do is have an honest discussion with yourself and ask yourself what tasks you don't want to do anymore. Once you start to set these boundaries for yourself, which is the hardest part, your commitment to higher value tasks will inevitably start to make you money. The cool part about training a virtual assistant is that all you have to do, is complete the tasks that you want to delegate one more time, but record them while you are doing them for the VA to watch.

A few pieces of advice here, go slower than you normally would when you record a video for your VA. Explain each step so that they really understand and have good instruction. If you are thorough in explaining, their chance of duplicating your success is much higher. You can use Loom, the free video recorder, to record these videos and share the link with your team. You can't expect what you don't inspect though, so use the following formula for successfully training your new team member:

1. Simplify your inner-office communication through a program like Slack (free). This way you can easily connect your virtual assistant with the rest of your team for streamlined communication and to give them a sense of involvement with the rest of the team.

2. Iron out the exact job description. It's hard to hold them accountable if you aren't giving them very specific tasks with thorough instruction.

3. Record yourself doing the task at about 70% normal speed, and explain each step. Their output is predicated on your input.

4. Have the virtual assistant complete the task on a practice run (or a few, to build some muscle memory for the task). Keep it fundamental, get them taking

more simple tasks off of your plate before you give them large tasks.

5. Have the virtual assistant complete the task on a live situation while you are observing

6. If number 3 went well, then delegate the task and check in periodically (more often to start until you trust them with your processes, then you can pretty much let go of the task). Try to keep the amount of tasks that you are delegating to three or less to start, so that they have the ability to develop a sense of comfort within them.

Wessly: *"You've got to find your pain points and your efficiencies that are being lost. The delegation and utilization of a virtual assistant really plays into being more efficient and being more productive. The two biggest fouls that I believe you could make if you own an insurance agency: Number two would be to pay your $17/hour team member to do a $10/hour task. That is bad business. You're essentially paying your head chef to bus tables. Number one foul is you as the owner doing those tasks. Whether you declare it or not, the action of that puts a valuation of $10/hour on your time."*

IF I WERE YOU: VAs will only be as good as how you train them to be. If your VA isn't reaching your goals, it's crucial to ask yourself if you are giving them the support that they need before you come down on them. Lead from the front, and they will follow.

Gratitude

One of the less expected but much appreciated outcomes of hiring virtual assistants is my renewed perspective on gratitude. I used to believe that all people operated on a "need" basis, and this was how the world worked. But when I hired my first virtual assistant, not only did they work harder than most people I have hired locally, every morning when they start their shift they reach out to me to express their gratitude for having this opportunity and for being a part of our team. It makes this feel special, but I'm far from alone on this.

The perspective it gives is that around the world, people generally have far less opportunity than Americans do and a lot of people here take what they have for granted. You'll rarely hear something like "Because I need a job" when asking a virtual assistant why they applied to work for you during an interview. They work incredibly hard, and it has deepened my respect for people around the world to see how much effort they give to the organizations they are a part of. Their gratitude has increased my gratitude, and in turn it's created a culture of gratitude that every new team member gets to participate in and it's contagious.

Wessly: *"Gratitude comes in and can consume your culture if that is the message that you start to infuse into your agency, but the same is true for entitlement. Both will spread if given space. People often ask me why I have so many virtual assistants. It's that gratitude."*

Experience for Yourself

Outsourcing and using virtual assistants is the solution for a bigger question you are asking yourself, which is, "What do I feel that my time is worth?" Then from there, finding ways to position yourself closer to your self-evaluation. If you have never asked these questions, you don't have to go at it alone. Wessly and AgencyVA (agencyva.com) have created a 25 point audit of your business to see where you can increase your efficiency and live the life that you want to live.

Wessly: *"Correct. What we advise for people to do is go through our 25 point audit. We'll briefly go over each task and ask "Who's doing this task? Is it sales, service or is it someone with ownership?" Then we put a numeric value next to each of those tasks. We go through all 25 and find the 3 biggest areas of opportunity that if we could help you solve, would make an immediate and huge impact on your business. You're leveraging a cost-effective solution to alleviate a profit-draining problem, it becomes a win-win situation."*

CHAPTER REVIEW: Outsourcing is about recognizing and realizing the hierarchy of your business. Whether you're the chairman of the board, whether you're the founder of a small agency, you need to have a hierarchal structure of delegation. Outsourcing makes it easy and cost-effective to build your company's structure to get the most production for your dollar.

UP NEXT: In the next section of the book, we will be going over topics that will help you scale your business with stable growth, and we're starting with your agency management system in the next chapter.

PART 3
<u>SCALE</u>

"Starbucks was founded around the experience and the environment of their stores. Starbucks was about a place with comfortable chairs, lots of power outlets, tables and desks at which we could work and the option to spend as much time in their stores as we wanted without any pressure to buy. The coffee was incidental."

– Simon Sinek

"When you're in a small boat, you can see who's paddling hard and who's looking around."

– Ev Williams

CHAPTER 10

You Need a Homebase
with Peter Germanov

In the first two parts of this book we focused on different methods to make more money and reclaim your time. The third part of this book is about integrating those techniques into your agency in a way that makes sense.

The first place to start is with your agency management system (AMS). This is where you will aggregate all of your client information, which allows for a wide variety of benefits that we will go over in this chapter.

One of the hot topics in the AMS world has been around potential for integration. You might have heard about API, or maybe you've heard the word "Zapier" being discussed. We will be going over simple ways to utilize your AMS to systematize your agency, as well as more advanced conversation about the importance of connecting your AMS to other platforms you are using to not only make your life better, but also to provide the best client journey possible. I am joined in this chapter by Peter Germanov, the founder of NowCerts –

which is the agency management system that I have been using for some time now.

The Data Revolution

We're in an interesting time where insurance agents are starting to realize that they could have better and more efficient agencies. We are starting to connect platforms together and we are looking for the best and easiest solutions for everyone involved. Agents want to connect and automate processes more than ever, but up to this point most AMS companies have severely limited an agency's ability to use their favorite software together.

The reason this is important is because the modern agency's ability to grow has to be directly tied to having efficient processes. Let me give you an example: Often times a prospect will call in for a quote to an agency, and the agent or CSR that answers the phone will start to write down some basic data gathering. They will fill out their quote sheet to the best of their ability and attempt to get as much information as they can to provide an accurate quote for the prospect, and then they will call them back. After they get off the phone, they have to enter this information into their computer. This is a pretty standard flow and most people do some variation of this.

Few agents use as little of a system as an excel spreadsheet, which at a small scale might get you by – but has massive E&O exposure potential at scale due to poor documentation, as well as a lot of wasted time trying to keep a spreadsheet cohesive and up to date.

Most agents use some form of a CRM (which stands for Customer Relationship Management) or an AMS, where they will then take the information they gathered and enter it into the system. If you're an independent agent, this might be your rater. But these systems only let you manually input data usually. If you wanted to build automated emails and text message into your agency to go out to prospects or clients, most of these AMS systems don't allow the connectivity to outside platforms as they are generally trying to sell a licensing fee to you for that access, or sell you their own version of that feature (which is usually less desirable).

This has been a struggle for the agents that are starting to leverage these tools because it cuffs the hands of progress in the individual agency, and the industry as a whole. This is one of the cool things about working with Peter and NowCerts is that I am extremely grateful for the level of consideration he gives to his clients needs with how they continue to develop the platform.

Peter: *"I'd like to start with one philosophical ground we've taken that differentiates us from other AMS systems. We have the luxury of being a relatively small organization which makes us much more flexible. We didn't want to reinvent the wheel. In other words, if another company is doing something better, say quickbooks for accounting or Infusionsoft for marketing automation, we're not going to build a CRM system or a full general ledger counting* *system. We will just plan on integrating. This gives our users the option. There's various tools, whether you pick a VOIP for your phones, or a rater for quoting, any type of application on the web... If our client is used to it, if they like that product, we're not going to force them to use our version of it, or any company we've partnered with. Clearly, the only choice was to open the system and to provide an open API, as well as a Zapier overlay for non-programmers, to be able to integrate any other web application out there, that they like and that they're familiar with and having success in using."*

Keeping It Simple

I want to make sure that I reduce these concepts down for people who are new to these kinds of ideas.

API is short for Application Programming Interface. Essentially, API makes it so that two different programs can communicate and can be used together. For instance, you can connect your VOIP system to your agency management system so when a client calls, if they are in your AMS they will display on your caller ID. One very simple example to explain this. When you hear or read about a software having "Open API", that means that specific program is willing to connect with other programs. Most AMS systems are not open, which is where problems start to arise.

Another term that you will hear is "Zapier", which is a software that you can use to connect two or more programs with Open API together, without having to know programming. Zapier acts as the translator. For instance, if you generate a lead on an online survey platform, you can "zap" that information over to another platform, say a Customer Relationship Management (CRM) system like Infusionsoft so that the system can start reaching out to the prospect automatically without you having to do anything. At the same time, I can "Zap" that information into NowCerts so that it's automatically in my Agency Management System without me having to do any data entry. It sounds complicated at first glance, but once you start to realize that you can automate most of the tasks that you do on a daily basis that remove you from communicating with people about insurance, you will start to realize how much money and time you could be saving.

What We Have to Gain

By connecting software together, you are making sure that things are consistent and accurate in addition to the time saving you experience. Let me give you a few examples, if you have a VOIP system, you can integrate that so that your calls are synced to your AMS. The call recordings can be stored for client files in the event that you need to recall a particular conversation. This can also allow for text messaging as well, which can also be logged to a client file. Maybe you want to integrate an automation platform like Infusionsoft or ActiveCampaign or FollowupTool (A service of Lightspeed Voice), you're able to make sure that you automate emails and texts to your clients based off of information in your agency management system.

For instance, imagine a renewal comes up for a client and you have connected your phone and automation platforms to your AMS, you will begin sending emails and texts to your client about their renewal without you having to lift a finger after the sequence is initially built. This frees you from all of those phone calls or emails that you would have had to make.

Peter: *"As most agents know, the easiest money in the business is when you keep your customers happy and you have to do as little as possible to keep them renewing. With a system like ours, policies can renew almost automatically with as little effort or input from the agent as possible, that's when you really make money."*

You can also integrate signature platforms, so instead of chasing clients down for ink signatures, you can email or text them eSignatures and since you can connect this software to your AMS, the signed documents would automatically import into that client file to keep it sorted well. You can integrate your email provider into your AMS, for instance if I have email conversation with a client, I can make sure that those conversations get stored in my clients' folder for recall if I need to in the future. Plus, it makes it easier to use my email. If you want to make it so that clients can fill out a policy endorsement request, or file a claim with your agency you can create a ticketing portal with a software like Freshdesk or Zendesk and embed this on your website, which will allow them to request these changes 24/7/365, and you could even have a Virtual Assistant (as we went over in the last changer with Wess Anderson) help complete the change request. Even as simple as integrating forms into your AMS. This makes it so you can have pre-filled Acord forms, or fillable PDF forms for fast data entry that you auto-upload into your AMS.

Think about all of the phases of your relationship with your client, where you could implement some of these things. Prospecting, new business, renewal, cancellation, claims, or any event that could use downloads from the carriers to trigger. There are a LOT of different things you can do with the right AMS, these are just a few examples to get you realizing the possibility of how your agency can evolve in a short amount of time with the available tools.

Peter: "When we owned an agency and created our own AMS to allow us some of these amazing features, that created this custom experience that almost completely freed up 2 of my 6 employees' workload. We we're able to grow in a lot of new ways because we weren't focused on repetitive tasks that, as we found, could be simplified or automated. That platform eventually became what NowCerts is today. Obviously, we sold the book to avoid conflict of interest, but all of this was inspired by clients who wanted to manage their own policies and have a more inclusive experience. Every one of these features cuts down on the amount of time an agent or CSR needs to spend in order to make an endorsement or change a policy. They got what they wanted, and we increased the productivity of all our personnel."

How to Take Action

If you don't have an agency management system currently, or maybe you've been on yours for a while and you know it isn't providing you with what you want, I understand that this may feel daunting. There are a lot of processes and people that exist to help you. Whether it's data migration from your current AMS to a new and better AMS, or leveraging a virtual assistant to help you transfer that data, or maybe just figuring out the first place to start, there are definitely options.

IF I WERE YOU: Go to nowcerts.com and request a free live demo, especially if you haven't ever had an AMS, this way you will get to see what software like this can do for you. They even have a version of the program that you can use to test the platform on your own to see if you like it. When I was looking to switch from my old AMS, this made it much easier for me to see exactly how I would be using it.

Another tip that I would pass to you if you are on Facebook, there is a NowCerts user group that you should join, it will help give you ideas on how to continue to evolve the software to your specific preferences. The reason I support this software (which in time will be called Momentum) is because it was the only platform that offered these kind of benefits without a massive licensing fee. As an independent agency owner having access to carrier downloads within my

AMS is necessary, and being able to trigger different automated events based on that data has helped us substantially.

CHAPTER REVIEW: Having a streamlined and personal experience will help give you the edge in a commoditized market driven by price – tools like a strong AMS give you the edge to be competitive. Remember that people seek price in the absence of value, and this is a great start to providing a valuable experience.

UP NEXT: We discuss how to keep your team inspired and working towards the agency vision with Jason Cass of Agency Intelligence.

CHAPTER 11

Your Biggest Asset (or Liability)
with Jason Cass

One of the biggest struggle points for a lot of agents is the churn of staffing. Not only the churn, but also the expense, especially when it's tied to the possibility of it not working out. It's way more expensive to rotate through staff than it is to pay them right the first time and keep them long term – and money's not the only factor.

As we discuss the need for good hiring and leadership practices within your agency, I am joined by Jason Cass who leads Agency Intelligence, a mastermind for insurance agencies, as well as his own independent insurance agency.

Our Evolution

Being a successful leader to attract and maintain your agency staff requires an understanding of our evolution as humans, which directly influences the way that we treat people. It's easy for us to take it for granted with all of the technological advancements around us, but it was less than 150 years ago that the light bulb was invented. Our culture has advanced exponentially, but in 150 years, or even 1,000 very little has changed biologically for us.

Jason: "Way back in the day, you'd see somebody across the plain and you didn't exactly know who they were, you would immediately seek protection with your bow or spear."

We learned quickly as a species, no one wants to be the first person to eat the poisonous berries, so we put up barriers to the unknown. The unfamiliarity or distance between people can cause a gap in trust, which is prevalent in many agencies across the nation. We're going to go over how we can rally the members of your team to be a part of the mission, and how to invite new people to join. It starts with getting to know the core desires of your team members, and how you can help them achieve those within the mission of your company.

Jason: "One of the cool things I learned about human psychology, is that most people will naturally work twice as hard to *keep something that they already have with certainty, than trying to work harder to gain something else that they aren't sure they'll receive. If I give you $50 and say "Here's $50, it's yours", you'll most likely say, "thanks, that's great man". But if I say, "Here is the deal, instead of the guaranteed $50, I'll give you $300 if you roll dice and get 7 or 11. If you win, you get $300, if you lose you get nothing." Majority of the time, people are going to want to keep the $50."*

Which makes sense, because historically humans are hunters/gatherers, and we don't know with certainty when our next meal will be. We are generally going to invest more time protecting the things we already have, than risk leaving the village to seek a better life. People die outside of the village.

Jason: *"Right, where this comes into play is your teams compensation. Often times agents will discuss team compensation and ask what is the ideal commission split, or should I do salary plus commission, but I want to propose a new way of thinking about this. Most agencies give someone a base wage of say $25 an hour, and then offer them a bonus of $5 an hour if they hit certain metrics. This hinges the success of their business goals on the production of their team when the team hasn't yet tasted the fruits of what the experience of success will be like. So, let's reverse this model. Tell them that they're going to get $30 an hour and you're expecting them to take ownership of the same metrics you wanted them to hit above, and if they don't hit them, they will have their pay reduced. What ends up happening is that the people who wouldn't have been* *motivated to work harder in the first place will just fall off, but your hard working staff that wants to win will work incredibly hard to defend what is now theirs."*

This is a great example of reframing your pay structure to help solve your teams core needs, which are universal for all humans. Let's review the six core human needs from Tony Robbins, and their relationship to your team:

1. Certainty: People need certainty in their lives for things like making sure they have enough money to pay their bills, feed their family, keep a roof over their head. Certainty is a huge driver in the workplace, especially when it comes to compensation because every team member likes to know what they're being paid, and when they're being paid that. People need a certain level of certainty to be able to live a healthy life.

2. Uncertainty: This is less obvious for a lot of people, but the counterweight need for certainty is uncertainty, or variety. A healthy life has both of these components. If you have too much certainty, then you experience a life of boredom. If you have too much uncertainty, you can lose your vision, direction of hope. So somewhere in the middle, people have enough certainty to have hope and direction, but also enough variety to keep them enthusiastic about the journey of life – or in your agency, about the

opportunity. Have you ever seen someone who seemed like they were always struggling through drama in their life and it was constant? Uncertainty might be their deepest need, because maybe the things that they are certain about are rooted in feelings of fear or pain.

3. Significance: People need to have meaning and purpose in their life. Knowledge that they matter. Significance carries multiple forms and people do great and horrible things to achieve significance. If you provide this to them within their position in your team, this can carry a team to far distant places as it is one of the deepest needs for most people.

4. Love and connection: This is absent in a lot of agencies, but people want to feel connected. Your team wants to have the ability to connect with each other, and to your clients. Providing an environment for the team to know that they are connected, and in some ways loved – works as its own form of currency. Like significance, this is one of the deepest needs of humans.

5. Growth: People need to know that they are better with each passing day. Physically, mentally and emotionally. Giving people an environment that not only allows for growth, but also encourages/ incentivizes it will be a solid foundation for your team to become the best version of themselves, which

in turn improves the business and the morale of the entire organization.

6. Contribution: People need to know that they have the ability, in some form to serve others and a purpose bigger than themselves. I feel like this is an undercurrent within most agencies, and the ones who embrace this within their staff will give their staff the freedom to really care and provide the experience the clients want.

There are many ways to be able to infuse these six needs into the compensation of the office, you can include these either in the metrics on which they are paid on, or the compensation that they receive. While money is a big motivator, it's by far not the only motivator to help your staff achieve a good life within your agency. Every person prioritizes these needs differently depending on their life experiences, so by getting to know your staff you can know what they are driven by, and help them meet their needs.

The first four needs everyone has and can help people charge through to victory. The last two needs are considered more spiritual needs, meaning when humans meet growth and contribution they feel fulfilled. Not everyone is seeking fulfillment, but if you can help people achieve their version of success within your mission, while giving them a platform to also be fulfilled – you will find the right compensation structure for your team members.

Jason: *"Here's another example, there's a grocery store out my way called Aldi's, they're everywhere out here in the Midwest now. They have all of grocery carts outside of the business because they don't have a lot of space. They're trying to keep things efficient. So, they put the carts outside, and they chain them all together. Each handle has a little chain, and when you want to use a cart you take a quarter and put it into the machine and it releases a cart. When you go to leave, you take your cart back up there and you connect it back to the rest of the carts, and your quarter pops back out. They don't have carts in their parking lot, it's cheaper than having to pay a staff person to chase carts down, but in reality – people don't want to lose their quarter. Since they had to give up the quarter to begin with, they want it back. Finding ways to let your team attach their work to your mission will make sure that everyone is closer to winning."*

Money Aside

Jason: *"It's interesting, there are a lot of behavior modifications that you can do. We have been talking about compensation, which usually starts with money. But my account manager and my receptionist, they don't really care about the money. What they want is to know that if they work hard, that they can have a half day on Friday to be with their family. They want to be able to pick their kids up rather than having the bus take them home."*

You can definitely see a desire for certainty, connection and contribution there, maybe even a fear of uncertainty. Fear of something can drive you just if not as the pursuit of it, often fear can be a bigger driving force in the choices you make.

Jason: "My sales guy has a whole different life with different motivating factors. He doesn't have a need to pick kids up from school, his life is different. To him, the money is a big motivator. So you have to know your team and what's truly important to them, understanding their core needs."

The desire for money might be certainty, it could also be uncertainty as well as significance of connection. You would know for sure by asking what he wants money to achieve.

IF I WERE YOU: Take time to connect with your team, and with yourself. Figure out what is important to each of you, what the desires are. If you have a staff member that wants to be able to work from home so that they can be with their children, this might mean that they are driven by connection and significance. Find ways to provide that to them. If they want money, maybe they are driven by certainty. If you ask what they want the money for, you will learn a deeper desire that will almost always expose the core need behind the desire for money. It's a great exercise to see what is driving you, and what is motivating (or not) your team.

Bringing it Home

After you understand the core needs of your team, it's important to tie in the ways you help them meet their needs with helping you advance your agency. By doing this, you can scale your growth by leapfrogging your time leverage.

For instance, let's assume you work 60 hours a week and you work 50 weeks a year. That's 3,000 hours per year. If you want to make $1,000,000 in a year, you divide the amount you want to make (1 million) by the time available (3,000 hours). That ends up being $333/hour. You and I both know that you can't make $333/hour if we are doing $25/hour tasks. So you need to hire someone to take simple things off of your plate, let's call them a CSR. You should eventually be delegating all of the $25/hour tasks to them and finding ways to attach the completion of those tasks to the core needs of your CSR, so now let's say that your time is worth $50/hour since you're doing higher level tasks, but eventually your CSR is becoming exhausted and exceeds their bandwidth, what do you do now?

You hire a CSR trainee and promote your CSR to an Agency Manager. You have them find the core needs of the CSR trainee are, and you build a compensation plan that helps them reach that goal while also taking over the former job of your ne Agency Manager. When you hire someone, and you connect their work to their core needs, you automatically give yourself a promotion. Now you're able to find what the next steps are in the life of your Agency Manager and how you can help her achieve those. Maybe they want more clearly defined expectations and accountability, this is often a less communicated need for team members as it takes a high level of EQ to acknowledge that is what you need, but it helps people meet their need of certainty because when they go to work, they know exactly what is expected of them. That gives them a target to aim at, and they know how to do their job so it becomes consistent for that person.

Keep promoting people to help you reach your goals, and you will do that by helping each person on your team meet their needs.

Jason: "It might sound crazy, but accountability has been huge for us. They want to be held accountable. They want to know that what they're doing is good. They want to know that they have work and purpose. They want to know that they are a strong role in our agency. I had a call with an agent recently and he said, 'I have a new young employee and I think they're going to be great, if they do their part they have a good future in this agency.' I said to him, "Do you understand how confusing that could be, if he does his part? Have you explained to him what his part is? Where he fits into the agency? Have you shared with them what it could look like one year, three years, five years? It's not just money. What's the type of lifestyle they want, and what do they want to achieve? You know that by asking those questions and letting them know that we can achieve that here. That creates stability, that creates security."

If you keep growing, and you give your team the same potential and are proactively trying to help them reach the growth they yearn for, that's when you achieve success. There's a definition of entrepreneurship that I subscribe to. It says that an entrepreneur is somebody who solves problems. When you look at it like this you start to realize that not all entrepreneurs are business owners. There are business owners that are not entrepreneurs, and there are entrepreneurs that are in the corporate world or work for a small business. The concepts in this chapter really orbit around the idea of fostering that entrepreneurship within your team.

Jason: *"There's a story that I really like that reminds me of this conversation. A CEO and a CFO are talking to each other about their employees and the CFO says to the CEO, "What happens if we train our people, and they leave?", and the CEO looks back at him and says, "What if we don't, and they stay?"*

CHAPTER REVIEW: When compensating your team, factor more than just money. Give them something to work hard to defend instead of tying them to goals that they haven't been able to experience the fruits of completing.

UP NEXT: We're going to dive into ways of deepening the culture of your agency with Zack and Matt of G&N Insurance.

The Agency with the Best Culture Wins
with G&N

When you are looking to implement changes to your systems, or with your team, everything impacts an element of how people perceive your brand. Clients, referral partners and team members alike, the way that people see you and how they act in the presence of your brand is what dictates culture. We're going to discuss methods to develop a strong culture within your agency, which directly applies to both small agencies and large ones.

To discuss this topic, I am joined by two masters of building winning culture, Zack Gould and Matt Naimoli. The owners of G&N Insurance and bobbleon.com which is the consulting platform from which they help agencies across the nation improve their culture and systems.

Matt: "A lot of the times people think about culture, they think about the environment you create. Safety, trust, transparency, etc. Those are all elements of culture, but one of the undervalued traits of good culture is the importance of structure within an agency. It's the actual steps in the process that will actually create the outcomes of an atmosphere that's trustful and that people are open and transparent and communicate. Who feel that they're heard and that they're not a number."

Respecting Strengths

When Zack and Matt decided to start their own independent agency, they had both already worked together at a large carrier as outside sales reps, and they knew that they could lean on each other to build their network as well as sell. Being able to lean on each other gave them the compounding effects of synergy, where 1 + 1 started to equal 3, and their growth was no longer just linear.

Zack: "We talk a lot about when that changed, but one of the key metrics of when that actually changed and when we realized we couldn't actually only be salespeople was when we brought on another outside producer who was not an equity partner, he was strictly an outside producer. He was so poorly managed because I didn't want to do it, and Matt didn't want to do it either, so we started to realize that we have to right this ship."

Matt: *"I think too, we didn't know what we didn't know. That's probably very similar to any other business owner out there who started anything from scratch or inherited anything for that matter. We were fortunate to be good at sales and to be able to get off the ground. Then once you're off the ground, you start to see momentum, like "wow, we can finally take some income, fantastic. Then, you're growing pretty fast, getting notoriety but the only want to break through ceilings at that point felt like working longer and harder. Zack and I would send each other emails at midnight or 2AM that were four paragraphs long because it was the only time we had. We were processing applications the entire evening, we were selling all day, we were networking all morning. There was no time to manage. We got to a point where we felt so much pain around the chaos, the business felt like it was owning us. We weren't owning the business. This was when we started doing some deep dive reflection on what we wanted to become moving forward and what our scale was and continued growth. What does that look like to us, because we certainly wouldn't be able to accomplish our goals long term if we continued on the same pace as we were."*

There's an element to building a business that is like driving a speedboat that's getting holes from the resistance of the water. If you're in the boat when that's happening, you have a few options. You can drive really fast and stay above the water, or you can focus on the holes. Successful business does both but if you're focused on speed and you're always on the go, you at least stay above water. But if you're always focused on holes, you don't move anywhere. There's a fine balance there where you have to start filling some of the holes while you're moving. That's where I feel like having solid processes can make a positive impact on your culture.

Matt: "At a certain point you can't make the boat go any faster. You have to focus on the holes. We're really grateful that we looked inward because our biggest growth, at least personally was that period of self-development and becoming a business owner. What does a business owner look like? When people say working on the business versus working in the business, what does that actually mean? People say it, but what do es that look like and translate to on a daily, weekly, monthly, quarterly, annual or even multi-year picture? That was part of our education. We became students of the business owner game and really tried to perfect ourselves in that process, elevating out of the business. That's been really the cause of the boat continuing to go super-fast while filling the holes."

Expectations and Agreements

Zack: "One thing that Matt and I focused tremendously on is the difference between expectations and agreements. That's with referral partners, that's with your team, that's also with your partnerships. To relate it in two different ways: If we went to a referral partner and said, "We expect you to refer X, Y and Z" they're not going to. If you go to your team and say, "We expect you to produce certain results and we expect..." you're going to have the same problem. We were managing our team with expectations but our referral partners with agreements. When we realized that we should manage and lead with agreements in both categories, we had excellent relationships with our referral partners and our team liked us, but I think more of who we were, not necessarily how we lead the team."

Expectation: a belief that someone will or should achieve something

Agreement: a negotiated arrangement between parties as to a course of action

Matt: "Yea, passion and enthusiasm can go a long way to galvanize support and get people on board to run with you, but to row in the same direction, you have to have a really strong structure and process. If you expect to continue to organically grow and do it fast without people quitting, without people giving their notice or yelling at one another, you've got to get the process structure. It felt like we mastered sales first, networking second, generally branding and marketing third and then process design. Structure, tools, resources, entrepreneurial tools and resources. We developed the entire operating system that G&N runs on so that we can actually sit here with you, fully interested and invested in the conversation and not worry about the 10,000 other fires going on around us."

IF I WERE YOU: Have a close look at how you communicate with your team, and ask yourself if you are holding them accountable to your expectations or their agreements? Are you giving them an environment where they are inspired to work hard to help you reach your vision for the agency? If not, I would have an open talk with your team about how this is important to you and you want to treat them better. They will very much appreciate your humility and transparency. If that is the environment you want, it starts with you.

Internal Pain

After consulting with over a hundred agencies over the last year and spending the time necessary to be able to make an impact on these agents lives, they started to realize that there was a lot of pain that these insurance agents were experiencing. These were similar pains from agencies all over the nation.

Matt: "We would get questions about business development, how to create more leads, referral partner questions. It could be questions about the sales process or service and renewal process or how to handle claims. All of these questions would come up and we would help people with them but we recognized that the foundational issue had nothing to do with us. That was the outcome. That was the external pain. The internal pain causing all these problems is that they didn't have a structure and a foundation to operate off of. Their operating system was non-existent. That's where we could relate because that's where we were for so many years. No matter whether they were selling 5 policies a week or 500 a week, we knew the pain that they were having. They didn't have an operational system and that's what we had mastered over the last few years. That's what we've been so excited about sharing with insurance agents and why we've been so eager to get across the country and work with people in person."

The issue has been similar for agents that we consult as well for lead generation or other marketing services when it's just by itself. Not all the time, but often someone may hire us to help them get leads, but when the agency gets leads they struggle to convert the leads which tells us that there is not necessarily a lead problem as much as there is a sales process problem. Fixing one component doesn't free the bottleneck in your business, it moves the bottleneck somewhere else and the key is to be able to keep your eye on the bottlenecks.

Matt: *"Yea, well said. When we experienced that we took a step back from business development. We took the foot off of the gas for 6 to 12 months so that we could focus on the nuts and the bolts, and get our systems dialed so that when we applied pressure again it would amplify without us feeling more pain. The results were awesome because our production went up, our lead gen ended up going up, our employee and client satisfaction levels went up and most importantly, our hours, when it comes to required hours being managed ourselves by the business went down. Our hours of actual entrepreneurship type work went way up because we had more bandwidth to do the things we loved to do."*

That's when Zack and Matt realized how crucial it is to have effective systems to support everything an insurance agency tries to implement, and how much that increased the overall happiness of their team. Often times agency owners will say things like, "It's so hard to find good people in the insurance industry". It's important that instead of waiting for the unicorn employee to show up, we help create a team of people who operate with systems that give them the super strength that we wish we could find. Every agency owner was at one point unlicensed, and we decided to dive in and create a business in this industry. So we also have to invest the resources to help our team grow to that. If team member turnover is high in your agency, focus on where you can make the experience better for the team – as that is often where the issues and gaps in your team relationships will arise.

A step in the right direction

Zack: *"I think that a lot of this comes from our weekly meetings that we talk about. This is one of the processes that we coach on that makes a massive shift in agency culture."*

Matt: *"Processes are a word that some may perceive as overused, but yet it's an undervalued and actionable element of your business. In our eyes, there are two sets of processes. One set is the client processes. These are what you do at every stage of the client lifecycle in your agency. We probably have over 60 of those written in checklist format in a proven process which yields the best desired results at every single stage. Whether it's business development, lead coordination, sales, service, claims, renewals, HR, finance, etc. The* *second set of processes are the ones that most people don't talk about, which are operating procedures. There's 25 to 30 that we operate off of. Meaning, when X happens, whether it's an issue, whether it's a protocol, whether it's development, whatever it might be, then Y is supposed to happen. These processes are one of the most successful things we've established in our business. Understanding what we are supposed to do when X happens and getting our team on the same page for that."*

Zack and Matt share one of their processes that helps them consistently grow and have an open culture of transparent communication. They wanted to share this with insurance agents so that agencies can start to connect with their team and work towards a common vision.

Matt: *"One of the very simple processes that we have which has made a profound impact almost immediately in our agency is our weekly structured meeting. Every week at the same time, same place, we meet for 90 minutes. It's structured specifically to act as a health checkup for that department whether it's a leadership team or any department at the agency. We all run off of the same format. Leadership team has their own weekly meeting. Sales has their separate meeting. Same for our marketing team, finance team, every team has a specific meeting, same structure but it's different people based on the accountability chart and the actual tree that we operate off of."*

Having each individual department meet separately allows for the teams to identify areas of improvement in their environment while doing so with high level conversation. Sales team doesn't need to know about finance issues, and marketing doesn't have to hear HR. This creates that honest and transparent open-format environment where team members can work together to solve the issues of the agency.

Matt: *"When we first started this it was Zack, myself and three other leadership team members. Part of this meeting is to specifically isolate and resolve issues that popped up. For the first three to four months that we were doing it, we probably had 25 to 30 issues that popped up weekly."*

Zack: *"It might sound like a lot, but think about what happens if you don't talk about issues the whole week. That's the thing. Nobody walks in Matt's door and is like, "Hey Matt I don't like how this is going down, how about you solve this." It gives the team permission to take the chance to solve things themselves. Failure is okay."*

Matt: *"Before we did this, we had 25 to 30 issues but they were the same issues that would hit us five times a day. We had fires all over the place. When we stopped doing that, no one came to anyone in the agency with issues unless it was massively urgent, really urgent, but most issues aren't that way. They're just things that are going wrong that need to be improved, need to be changed. Everyone started to compile their issues in a shared folder and address them together once a week. That was stage one. Stage two is when everyone in the entire agency and each department was running these meetings, the beauty was that the leadership team only had two to four issues because 20-25 of the agency issues would normally be resolved in the foundational levels. The sales team, the service team, accounting, all these teams are creating solutions for their own problems. They didn't bubble up on us."*

It's cool to see how what was an attempt to give structure to a team and streamline efficiency within the agency ended up also automating the leadership development for the business as well.

Zack: *"It's interesting Preston. You talk about why people leave teams, people leave teams because of managers, not because of companies. No one is going to leave Amazon because they found out it wasn't really Amazon. They leave because of their manager. Great companies don't have that problem because they care. They show that they care. Great managers care, not necessarily just by finances, not necessarily by benefits, not necessarily by time off or the ability to work from home. Great managers show that they care because they listen and they act. They hold people accountable."*

Matt: *"It's hard to do that without structured processes and tolls in place throughout the week to support your team. When we break down our weekly structured meeting, the first 20 minutes is a health checkup in every way. We start with an ice breaker and that creates an open line of communication with everyone on the team where we focus on the top personal highlight that happened in the last seven* *days. Zack could say he had a great experience with his son Mason, had an awesome time at the museum of science or something and I could say something else personal and go around. It creates that atmosphere where everyone is very open."*

IF I WERE YOU: Start grouping the agency issues together for a weekly 90-minute review. This way you aren't being steered by the nose every time an issue comes up. You have a dedicated time weekly to address, isolate and solve the issues. During the week, you put the issue in the folder to be discussed later instead of operating with anxiety every time a new problem comes up, which will kill your production.

Money's Not Enough

You can't buy culture, it has to be earned. When agents talk about what they think will attract a good team member you can see them discussing the ideal pay structure. What should their commission split be, or should it be salary plus commission? There are really three things that can dictate your team's experience for compensation: Money, time off, and recognition. All three can take vastly different forms which vary depending on the person. I think a new form of compensation is also feeling connected, we call it culture, but people like to be a part of something bigger than themselves. People like to know they're pulling their way, it gives a sense of accomplishment and purpose towards the vision.

Matt: *"I think a lot of employees across the country in five person shops and 40,000 employee companies feel that way. We both feel this way, it's more than compensation, it's more than perks, it's more than any of that stuff. It's accountability and autonomy. People want to be held accountable because they want to be able to judge if their input is creating the intended output. They want to know if they're doing a good job. There's a different level of recognition between just being held accountable, and being told, "Hey, you're achieving the results that we set out for you and that's a great thing. It means you're putting a lot of effort in, and we see and respect it." The other piece is autonomy. They want to know that if they have an issue, there is a structured way every week where they can submit that complaint, issue, vent it out, identify with the team, resolve it right then and there together instead of sending it in an email to the intranet and hoping HR will solve it in six months. There's a huge difference."*

Zack: *"The other thing that Matt was hitting on is that everybody also has a number which is really important too, in the entire organization from the assistant to Matt and I. What I mean by that, it's a number that you can control. Not a number that we expect you to do. If you think about that number, the employee agrees with the manager, I agree that I am held accountable to this number. This goes back to agreements over expectations. If I can't hit my number, I might as well not have a job. It's that important of a weekly number. Over time we look at the average of that number, and assess whether we are hitting it or not. The number, the category is semantic and will change for every agency. It has to be specific to* *every agency and support the mission of that business. We also make sure that every team member knows and experiences a ton of recognition when they're hitting the number that's supporting the mission of the company. It helps them feel incredibly valued."*

It ties into the concept that an army can't siege a castle without a king. Every part of that army is critical to success because if the soldiers fail the king has to fight and if the king dies then the war is lost. Every person wants to be a part of something bigger than themselves, and this system allows you to tap into that core human need. When the war is over, and we have won people want to be part of the crowd that stands on top of the hill holding the flag.

Matt: *"Yea, the more valuable each person feels to accomplish that mission, the better. I think that's why our retention with employees is so high even though they work their tails off, it's because they each feel so valuable, they are measured as Zack said, on the things that really matter for the agency. It's not happenstance."*

Zack and Matt have taken their processes and started to consult agencies on these different systems that they use to be successful and build a massive culture. If you haven't been following G&N Insurance on social media, I would highly recommend it. They're awesome people and that's why I am grateful to be connected to them.

CHAPTER REVIEW: Culture is built on the foundation of strong agency processes. If you fail to have consistency in the initiatives you make with your agency, it's most likely because there is an underlying process issue. Start to focus on your processes and the issues will be minimized because you have streamlined how you solve the problems and the team knows what is expected of them.

UP NEXT: The conclusion of this book and the next step in your journey to implement these strategies into your agency.

Conclusion

Digital Natives Academy

After going through this book, you have learned about a lot of new and exciting techniques and strategies that you can implement in your agency to start seeing growth right away. I can imagine if these concepts are new to you, you are likely overwhelmed right now.

You should be proud of yourself, you just completed what is essentially a deep-dive and immersive course on how to bring your insurance agency into modern times, which for most people is no small feat. Being overwhelmed is a part of the process.

On the other side of this information, your brain will start to look at your problems differently. Your solutions will seem more innovative. Your relationship with your team should be improved. You may not notice it right away, but you've now witnessed many new and improved ways to do business, and see the world.

When you are deciding what you should take action on first, here's what I would recommend from my professional experience:

1. Make sure that you really know what your unique offer is to your clients.
2. Identify your ideal clients.
3. Create a marketing plan with the information in this book to connect with your ideal clients.
4. Out of all the strategies in that plan, choose the one thing that if you make progress on it will make a significant improvement in your agency.
5. Focus and start implementing on that one thing.
6. Complete that strategy before moving onto the next one.

The intention behind this book was to give you a guide that you can read through from start to finish, or come back for "as needed" information while you keep growing your business. Keep it close to you through your journey so that you never have to be isolated or stagnant. My recommendation is to spend the next few weeks implementing the techniques that we go over in this book. Your time to improve your life is now, you don't have to wait anymore to live a more free and prosperous life with your dream agency.

Over the last year, I have travelled to help agents all over the nation solve these very issues that we discuss in the book, and I am happy to be able to share these ideas with you that we implemented for them while I was consulting their agency. Every agent who we consulted on these principles saw dramatic increases in their business. They generated more revenue, they had more time, and they scaled more efficiently. That's the purpose of this book.

As we distribute this book, I realize that I will have less bandwidth to help so many agents, so that's why we created the Digital Natives Academy where we consult insurance agencies on all of the different subjects within this book and directly help them implement these strategies. They work, they are highly actionable and easy to apply with guided help, and they change lives.

To make sure that I can offer personalized consulting and coaching to agency owners, those who have read this book, we have opened up space in our Digital Natives Academy consulting program so that I can personally build an action plan to implement all of these systems over the course of a year. My team and I give hands on assistance and training to teams in our program, we help implement systems to alleviate the headache and lost time of trying to figure it out. It's the fastest way to compete at the top with your agency.

If you'd be interested in forever improving your agency and being a part of the Digital Natives Academy, then I want to invite you to join me personally. You can do so here:

www.digitalnativesacademy.com

After you apply, you will speak to a member of my team to go over your agency goals and our program to see if it's a good fit to work together. If it is, then we will discuss and map out an action plan for your agency to reach new heights.

Thank you so much for reading, I hope this book has served you and I wish you massive success.

Preston Schmidli

Tech Reference

Relevant Technology for Insurance Agencies

We wanted to make sure that this book would be as timeless as possible, to work towards that goal, we have compiled a list of technology and service companies for the insurance industry to help you implement the strategies within this book.

We understand that over time, these things may change before we issue a new version of this book. To relieve that problem, you can go to **ifiwereyoubook.com/resources** to get an up-to-date list of these categories to help your business.

Agency Marketing and Sales Consultation:
Digital Natives Academy – digitalnativesacademy.com
Fully comprehensive consulting to guide agencies through implementing all of the techniques within this book with an emphasis on sales and marketing systems through proprietary processes.

Video Marketing Education:
Made You Look Marketing – madeyoulookvideo.com
Training that is helped to teach business owners how to leverage marketing with an emphasis on video inside of their business.

Websites:
Advisor Evolved – advisorevolved.com
Website development and tools that help independent agencies and wealth advisors save time and money on service work, and generate consistent new business opportunities.

Quoting Proposals:
Neoteric Agent – neotericagent.com
Create modern insurance proposals that clients love
AdvisorEvolved – advisorevolved.com

Outsourcing:
AgencyVA – agencyva.com
A virtual assistant firm that helps insurance agencies run more efficiently by delegating tasks to outsouced team members. AgencyVA's goal is to help insurance agents experience freedom.
Coverdesk – coverdesk.com
Marblebox – marblebox.com
Upwork – upwork.com
OnlineJobs – onlinejobs.ph
Fiverr – fiverr.com

AMS:

NowCerts – nowcerts.com

A full-featured, cloud based agency management system that offers everything an independent agency needs to manage its business effectively for a fraction of the cost of what the legacy AMS charge. We have exceptional customer service and we are the only AMS that offers a truly open API. Intelligent, Secure, Intuitive, Innovative!

Hawksoft – hawksoft.com

EZLynx – ezlynx.com

QQ Catalyst – Vertafore.com

Tech Canary – techcanary.com

VOIP/Phone Systems:

Lightspeed Voice – lightspeedvoice.com

Enabling companies with unique state-of-the-art communication tools and an unprecedented view into the life of your business.

RingCentral – ringcentral.com

DYL – dyl.com

ZipWhip – zipwhip.com

Bluewave – yourbluewave.com

The Kotter Group – kotter.net

Automation:

Infusionsoft – Infusionsoft.com

ActiveCampaign – activecampaign.com

Salesforce – salesforce.com

Hubspot – hubspot.com

Zoho – zoho.com

Referral and Review Generation Platforms:
Rocket Referrals – rocketreferrals.com
Podium – podium.com
Lift Local – liftlocal.com
Magnfi – magnfi.com

Answering Services:
Answer1 – answer1.com
Insure Response – insureresponse.com

Sales Management Software:
Pipedrive – pipedrive.com
Salespype – salespype.com
Velocify – velocify.com
AgencyZoom – agencyzoom.com

eSignature Softwares
InsureSign – insuresign.com
SignNow – signnow.com
HelloSign – hellosign.com
DocuSign – docusign.com

Scheduling Platforms:
Acuity – acuityscheduling.com
Calendly – Calendly.com
ScheduleOnce – scheduleonce.com
x.ai

Landing Pages:
Clickfunnels – clickfunnels.com
Leadpages – leadpages.net
Instapage – instapage.com

Form/Survey Software:
SurveyGizmo – surveygizmo.com
Gravity Forms – gravityforms.com
Wufoo – wufoo.com

Agency Communication:
Slack – slack.com
Glip – glip.com
Microsoft Teams – Microsoft.com

Ticketing Software:
FreskDesk – Freshdesk.com
ZenDesk – Zendesk.com
Hubspot – hubspot.com

Made in the USA
Middletown, DE
09 January 2020